ENNEAGRAM

A step by step guide to discover the secrets of your true spiritual personality, to create healthy and lasting relationships in love, friendship and work - it includes a test of the 9 personalities types).

TABLE OF CONTENTS

INTRODUCTION

Today's world sometimes appears strange to you, sometimes complex to understand. It's not always easy to do the right thing or choose the roads that can lead you to happiness or the future you want. This is because each person must interface with many other individuals in an intricate tangle of relationships, people, unexpected events.

The first step to stay healthy and achieve your goals is to know yourself and understand all the potential of something has always been within your human body: your consciousness. Men and women are indeed wonderful and extremely powerful creatures but they do not always know how to exploit their weapons and their most hidden treasure.

This book is much more than an informative book or a self-help book. This is a business card for the outside world and for self-awareness. I will guide you on an accurate path and when you reach the end of the last page I am sure you will sigh, look in the mirror and say that you can finally go out and start living.

The set of automatisms, more powerful, more cohesive than the human being is precisely what is called the character, which is experienced subjectively as doing "what comes naturally to do": on the one hand it is our workhorse and on the other hand it is our destiny, our prison. The character is neither something to be erased nor something to be proud of. The automatisms are sometimes useful and sometimes not: it is a matter of knowing them and, if necessary, signing them or deciding that it is time to disconnect the autopilot. The problem is that, if you don't notice that there is, the autopilot cannot be disconnected.

Maybe you think that these things I'm telling you are only about the most mental sphere of your life, but it's not like that and to let you understand I want to tell you the story of two Zen monks walking on a muddy road.

"Two Zen monks called Eiji and Momo, were walking along a muddy road after a storm. Immediately after a bend they noticed a beautiful girl on one side of the road she had to cross to get to the other side. This beautiful girl was wearing a kimono and a silk scarf and he was very afraid of getting these precious robes dirty, for he showed all his hesitancy in crossing the street.

The two monks approached.

"Come, girl," Eiji said and picked her up to carry her across the street.

Once the girl was helped, the two monks continued in silence. But Momo had a thought that did not abandon him.

Five hours later, in the vicinity of the temple that would host them, Momo could no longer hold back the thought that had been crowding his mind for hours: "We monks do not approach women," he tells Tanzan, "and least of all those young and pretty. It's dangerous. Why did you do that?

Tanzan looked at Ekido and calmly replied, "I left that girl down there hours ago. Why are you still carrying her? "

Do you understand the meaning of this story?

It is not important what happens to you in life but your mental attitude. No matter the rest of the world, what really matters is you, your brain and how you deal with your life situations.

What is an enneagram?

Enneagram comes from the words ennea and gramma or 9 and sign and means nine-point drawing. The enneagram is a true theory of personality, which boasts ancient origins. However, psychologist Oscar Ichazo in 1970 valued it as a psychological tool. According to this theory there are 9 different types of personalities, namely the enneatypes, each with its peculiar characteristics. The peculiarity of the resulting instrument lies in the fact that the types of personalities are not static, but dynamic. This means that the resulting encyte type would then be like a photograph of a single moment of our life; through our growth path, however, we will probably move from one category to another, emphasizing and modifying certain aspects of our personality, such as beliefs, behaviors, feelings and emotions.It is also important to bear in mind that particular conditions, such as stress, can affect the resulting encephalty.

The Enneagram describes in a surprisingly precise way different aspects of human experience and nine different types of characters, each with specific mental, emotional and sensory patterns. We can define character as that pattern of beliefs, emotional attitudes and habitual behaviors that we call "myself".

1. The Type One likes to do things the right way, is a hard worker, honest, self-critical and easily frustrated

2. The Type Two loves to help others is passionate, devoted, capable of sacrificing itself for those who love and are easily intrusive
3. Type Three loves to win, it is brilliant, active, practical and often obsessed with image
4. Type Four loves to express itself in a free and original way, is creative, refined, lover of art and often self-centered
5. Type Five loves autonomy and solitude, is attentive, thoughtful, intense and often not very demonstrative.
6. The Type Six loves friendship and being gregarious, is faithful, committed, legalistic and easily skeptical
7. The Seven Type loves fun and variety, is cheerful, optimistic, hedonistic and is often superficial
8. The Type Eight loves to decide for his own life, he is combative, resourceful, determined and easily authoritarian
9. The Nine Type loves peace, is calm, patient, conciliatory and easily lost in his own world

HONESTY IS IMPORTANT

In this chapter I will talk about honesty and the importance of recognizing yourself in a complicated system of relationships and events.

Do you think you are honest with yourself?

Being honest is always the best solution. In fact, to tell the truth, even when it is hard and painful, leads people to trust us faster. Honesty is the basis of every healthy relationship, it makes relationships stronger, and at work it allows us to build a better environment, more serene, which helps us to be more productive. In a world where only the clever and recommended seem to be advancing, dishonesty may appear to be winning, but it is not really so. The dishonest may indeed have advantages in the short term, but in the long run it is the honesty that is recognized and that makes us live better. The honest are in fact healthier - a study has shown that lies cause tension, nervousness, physical pain - and have a better reputation. Despite the obvious advantages of honesty, however, being sincere with ourselves and others is not always easy, but rather, as every good practice needs exercise. Here are three simple steps that will help you be honest at work.

1. Be kind, first of all with yourself

Honesty is closely linked to kindness. Being dishonest increases blood pressure, and therefore stress; it also leads us to doubt our self-esteem, to seek self-gratification that often catapult us into a spiral of lies, from which it becomes increasingly difficult to get out. On the other hand, being honest means first of all being kind to yourself: it's the best way to start taking care of our health.

2. We work on our way of being honest

To be honest, say how things really are, sometimes you have to be tough but that doesn't mean that honesty should always be brutal. First we need to ask ourselves if our honesty really has good intentions, or if we are taking advantage of it to punish indirectly who we are facing. Before being honest, we must always ask ourselves: is my honesty true? It's necessary? And kind? If the answers to these questions are affirmative, there is no more doubt, the person with whom we will be honest will thank us.

3. Let us reflect on the effects of dishonesty

You should know that a series of precautions can help you resist when you are tempted to engage in dishonest behavior. According to the results of the experiments of the authors of the research, honesty would be a bit like a diet, that is difficult to follow without keeping in mind the objective (the advantages of honesty) and above all without considering the negative consequences of one's actions dishonest in the past. To be honest it can therefore help you reflect on the deleterious effects of an unethical attitude, but also learn to recognize and identify the situations that could put us in the situation of having to lie.

In a world where dishonesty seems almost commonplace and is often predicted to be part of "making success", why should a person be honest? Wouldn't it be naive and stupid? Wouldn't people take advantage of an honest person?

Honesty is connected to many things and affects our lives in many ways. Honesty expresses both respect for oneself and respect for others. Dishonesty respects neither others nor themselves. Honesty permeates the life of frankness, reliability and candor; it represents a disposition to live in the light. Dishonesty seeks the shadow, cover and hiding places. It is a disposition to live at least partially in darkness.

Honesty means telling yourself and others the truth, even if it is sometimes difficult. Honesty is much more than just not lying, it is a sincere devotion to the sense of truth. An honest person seeks the truth with an open mind and tries to communicate the truth clearly. Honesty begins within us, is part of our personal relationships and eventually colors and directs everything we do.

Honest people are trustworthy. They can be relied on, they are what they say they are, they want to say what they say and keep their word. The level of honesty with which we live influences our whole life, from our relationships with others to our image of ourselves. Honesty is a personal virtue possessed by many of the great people in history and by those who are working to achieve a higher realization of themselves.

Why is it often so difficult to be honest? Why can anyone think of being dishonest?

If we think about it honesty is important for everyone. A society based on deceit and lies cannot function well. If we cannot believe that the people around us tell us the truth, our sense of community suffers. Deceptions and lack of trust lead to conflict and social disintegration.

Of course, listening to the truth is not always easy. Leaders often surround themselves with people who tell them what they want to hear instead of what they should hear. Hearing the truth means we may have to change something we'd rather leave as it is. The truth often exposes our selfish side that we would not want others to see. This is because the truth is often assimilated to light. Light makes things appear that are hidden in darkness. When the dishonesty of enlargement is allowed, the whole society suffers and eventually declines.

We all have some dark side that negatively affects us and that, in a sense, is a self-defense strategy chosen unconsciously to achieve security and satisfaction and to avoid pain and failure. Recognizing the secret dominance of these negative impulses is the first step towards inner freedom. The enneagram, an ancient doctrine that is rediscovered and appreciated today by theologians and psychologists, can be an effective means of acquiring the necessary capacity for self-criticism in view of a more harmonious psychological and spiritual growth.

The enneagram is a doctrine that describes nine different characters. But in addition to the detailed description of the various human characteristics, the enneagram leads to internal and external change. The enneagram is more than a psychological investigation for self-knowledge, it gives us the possibility of confronting ourselves with the automatism in which we live unconsciously, invites us to become aware of it and to move towards freedom.

The enneagram defines nine types of personalities starting from nine 'traps', 'passions' or 'mortal sins'. These are the seven deadly sins: pride, envy, anger, sloth, avarice, greed, lust, and to these are added two more 'sins': lies and fear. The term "sin" is understood as our "separation from God", but also from our neighbor and from ourselves. "Sins" are exacerbations of the character that prevent energy, God's love, from flowing freely. We have chosen every "sin" and therefore we are responsible.

Each of the nine personality types includes a class that extends between extreme poles: "irredento" (immature, unhealthy) and "redeemed" (mature, healthy). An unredeemed person is imprisoned in himself, and thinks that his point of view is the only valid one.

The Sufis called the enneagram 'The Face of God', they imagined that in the path of liberation man becomes more and more capable of abandoning his position to observe life from another point of view. If we were able to 'wear all nine pairs of shoes' and observe reality from each of the nine points of view, then we would observe the world with the eyes of God.

On the opposite bank we find the 'redeemed personality'. The closer we get to God - the center to which we tend - the more we move towards the redeemed part. A great help in this sense is the community, the group. None of the nine types is better or worse than others, each of them needs to reach freedom and each of them has unique gifts.

Knowing the Enneagram it is possible to better elaborate our relationships and the dynamics of relationships: in the workplace; between parents and children; between men and women; of friendship; of group. But above all, the enneagram is a very useful tool for self-knowledge and self-awareness.

Enneagram helps us to identify the forces we need to cultivate and shows us the direction to follow by developing the positive qualities of our personality type. In this way the enneagram is very useful because it helps us to understand our strengths and our weaknesses; it helps us to know what price we will have to pay in the long term if we continue to enlarge our "I" and shun growth and it helps us to know with certainty that there is a "positive" way of living. If we want our change to go in the direction of growth, we must learn to desire what is truly right for us and have the courage to rebel against our fears.

The Enneagram is a map, a powerful tool for supporting self-knowledge and understanding others.

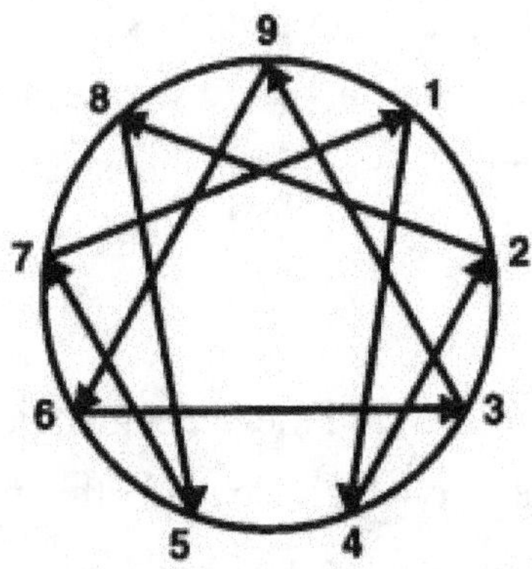

The Enneagram helps us to recognize ourselves and see others as they are, to understand and discern our experience, to discover and honor our natural talents and take responsibility for our difficulties in relationship problems, to manage conflicts in a way constructive, to overcome the lack of trust and find strength in themselves, to have less fear and to love more. All this without calculation and without guru, the only ingredient needed is openness to being honest with oneself.

The Enneagram is formally represented by a circle that includes an equilateral triangle intersecting a six-sided figure. The points that touch the circle are numbered from one to nine in a clockwise direction and are connected by lines and arrows in both internal figures.

The Enneagram is a true map of the psychological aspects and to describe nine types of personalities with distinct and specific mental models that then flow into emotional and sensory aspects, and their predisposition and ways of meeting and coordinated action. It explains the true motivations of our behaviors and reveals the intentions and beliefs that often automatically guide our choices.

In reality it is much more. It is also a map that describes different aspects of human experience and natural forces that exist within us all and the journey that every human being can take on their journey home, of self-remembering.

The Enneagram is recognized as the most powerful and practical intercultural system available for personal development and professional growth in any area and area of life. It is a system that improves any type of relationship, refines communication, educational method, therapeutic orientation, offers the possibility of positive management of feedback and conflict.

Its peculiarity is the ability to bridge the gap between psychological and spiritual development. Indicates in a clear and detailed way the real motivations of people's choices and behaviors, illuminating natural talents and areas for improvement of different character styles and providing concrete specific development strategies for each of them.

The body of knowledge of the Enneagram is an incredible concentration and integration of philosophical and mathematical understandings of different ages, cultures and traditions. Regarding the symbol, the origins are lost in history. The first to introduce it in the West was the Armenian Georges Ivanovitch Gurdjieff around 1913 using it to describe the cosmic order of the universe and creative processes. He spoke of the existence of dominant character traits in each individual, stating that "Essence is truth in man, personality is lie". In 1955 the Bolivian anthropologist Oscar Ichazo interpreted the symbol he called enneagono to describe nine types of people and the vicissitudes of the initiatory journey into themselves. In 1968 he founded a School for Awakening in Arica, Chile. In the 1970s his pupil Claudio Naranjo, a Chilean psychiatrist, reworked the basic descriptions of the types in character models, calling them enneatipo. Many names from those years have contributed to the dissemination, development and adaptation of the original theory.

"There are minds that question themselves, that desire the truth of the heart, seek it, strive to solve the problems generated by life, seek to penetrate themselves and the essence of things and phenomena. If a man thinks and thinks well, no matter what path he follows to solve these problems, he must inevitably return to himself and begin by solving the question of what he himself is and what his place is in the world around him. - G. I. Gurdjieff -

The original theory of the Enneagram states that psychological structures arise as answers and strategies to manage the illusion of detachment from aspects of the divine nature towards which one is particularly receptive and sensitive. This leads to nine different incomplete perceptions of reality that become distorted and fixed beliefs about how things are and that underlie the nine types.

And so here a new perspective is formed and a better vision of oneself and of the neighbor inserted in the generic world of today and tomorrow, the distorted aspects of the character that operate automatically are the ways of access to our natural abilities.

The Enneagram also identifies three Intelligence Centers in the human mind. The center of the bowel that allows us to act, the seat of instinctive intelligence and memory of the body, the center of the heart that allows us to desire, the seat of emotional intelligence and the center of the head that allows us to know, the seat of cognitive intelligence.

Each center includes three types and has a specific dominant energy, a particular aspect that it has difficulty managing. The anger for the center of the bowels, the shame for the center of the heart and the fear for the center of the head. The three points corresponding to the corners of the inner triangle are the nuclear points of each Center.

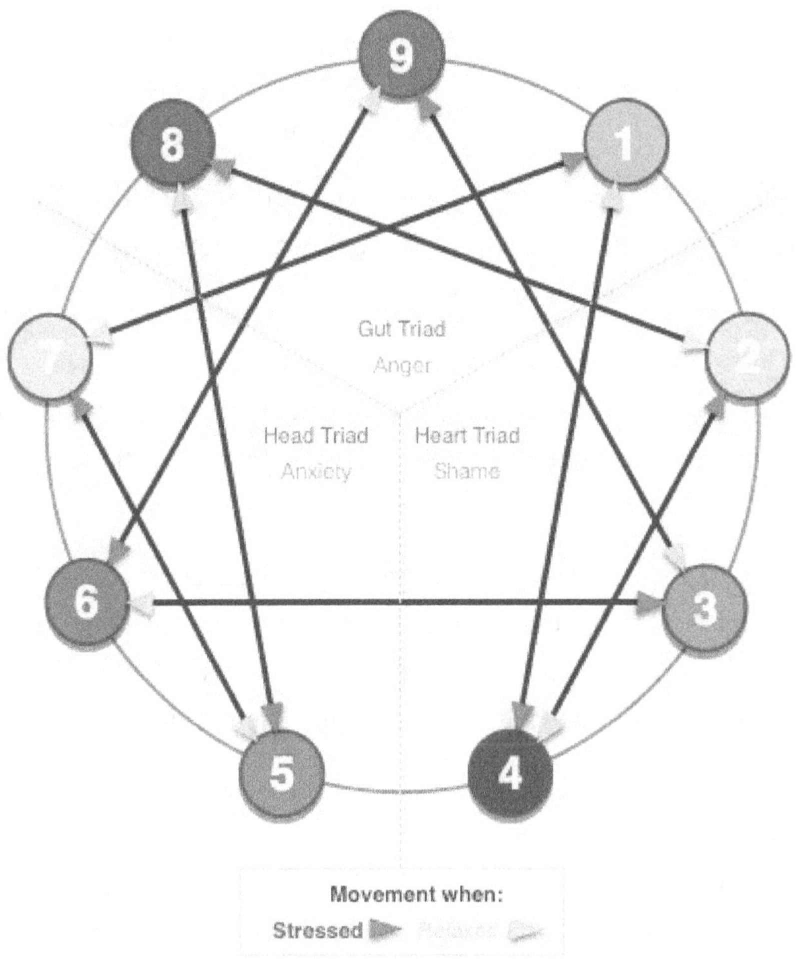

The Enneagram offers numerous levels of interpretation and two of them are particularly evident. The first allows the recognition of ego patterns and their predictability. A second and deeper function of the Enneagram leads beyond the personality into the realm of essence and self, becoming a model of consciousness that indicates the existence of the personality as a veil over the essential self.

The Enneagram is an instrument of transformation because information acts in the space of consciousness. It is an invaluable tool in the process of rediscovering our true identity.

To really improve the quality of our life and because the contact and expression of our talents are stable, much more than interesting information on the nine types is needed.

This soul map becomes functional and really useful when it is inserted in a context and is practically integrated with a practice, with an attitude of love for the truth, openness and respect for the mystery of life.

One of the great strengths and interests of the Enneagram is its being objective, not embracing a particular ideology and placing doctrinal differences outside. This helps individuals of religious faith, belief, education and culture to rediscover the fundamental unity that makes us similar.

The Enneagram can therefore be of enormous value in the contemporary world to show how, looking beyond the superficial differences that separate us, we can discover and meet each other at a level of common humanity.

Do you need to be honest at all costs? Does being sincere really mean asserting the truth? How to teach to be honest? Why is it important in a relationship?

The sincere person is someone who expresses what he feels and what he thinks, without conspiracy, this does not mean that he affirms the absolute truth, he is rather a pure person, open, without filters, but educated and respectful and at the same time courageous. The sincere person is pure, he does not use tricks in dealing with others. A sincere person is with words but even more with intentions and his way of doing things. He can also lie in order not to hurt and remain a sincere person.

Those who are sincere are not afraid of being judged, they do not want to like at all costs, they know how to use suitable words and choose the right moment to express their opinion without hurting because "Words have the power to destroy and to create. When words are sincere and kind, they can change the world "(Buddha)

It is a person who has the qualities of purity, frankness and clarity, certainly not the brazenness for the sake of saying all that comes to mind, without restraints. The sincere person does not feel the need to deny something and takes responsibility for what he says, hypocrisy and lies are not part of his life.

We are not interested now in knowing whether or not it is objective truth, the one told by a sincere person, but we are interested in knowing how sincerity is important in a relationship of any nature. In any relationship it is not so important if what you say responds to absolute truth, you tell us your truth, what you feel at that particular moment, what you think, what you carry, what everyone can assume their responsibilities but that will probably not be true forever.

To be honest we have to work on ourselves, get used to dig into ourselves, make our thoughts, but also the emotions and feelings we feel, easily manifested to let us know, to make others share in our ideas and our personal truth, to allow others to fully understand each other without doubts and without giving rise to inaccurate interpretations. Sincerity is important if you want others to learn to trust you. A sincere person is self-confident, so he does not need to deceive or betray the trust of others.

The observer learns in turn to be sincere and the relationship will cement. In the end, sincerity is the quality we would most like our friends, family, colleagues, all of us to have. We must learn, to teach later, to be honest. It will be enough to show ourselves as we are, to resist the temptation of wanting to appear different from what we are, only in this way could we reach the heart of those we love. To show ourselves for what we are, even if we do not feel perfect, strive to be honest with ourselves, engage in the things we feel we do and not because we have been asked by others. Just learn to talk about yourself, or express your opinion on any topic, with extreme spontaneity and following the heart. Make sure that others have no doubts about our intentions and so, soon, they will be in tune with our way of doing. We must train ourselves to be friendly, to smile, not to show off at all costs, as well as to consistency. Because being sincere, with tact and respect, always pays.

If you are sincere, those around you will not be slow with you.

If you want your child to be sincere, you must be honest with him, you must be able to listen to anything, without expressing your disappointment or your fears, you must be open to everything and try to listen without interrupting, until you will ask your opinion, and it is not said that it will. If you really have to tell him something, or you don't like long breaks, show yourself happy that he has confided his thoughts to you. Don't show yourself intransigent, if a child senses what arguments you would never share, which scandalizes you, he won't talk to you anymore and will look for someone to listen to him without criticizing or not expressing opposition. Then it will be difficult to bring him back to you for his confidences.

Speaking of sincerity, it is also important to understand what lies you usually hear every day. Here is a small Focus on how to recognize lies.

The eyes
Liars trying not to look away even in an ostentatious way to avoid losing focus on you and your way of getting their lie. Generally, people who tell the truth move their eyes and can even look away from time to time. Liars, on the other hand, will use a cold and constant look to intimidate and control.

Breathing
The slow and heavy breathing is a reflex action, almost uncontrollable when you tell lies.

The position of the head
Liars are prone to sudden head movements when you ask them a direct question.

The mouth
A person's mouth often dries while he is lying.

The movement of the body
People get upset when they get nervous, but according to experts you should also look at people who don't move at all.

The repetitions
The one who lies consists often repeats the same sentences validating the lie in their mind.

The amount of information
When someone definitely gives you too much information compared to those requests, enriched by a great deal of detail, there is a high probability that he or she is not telling the truth.

THE NINE TYPES OF THE ENNEAGRAM

As you will have understood, the Enneagram of psychological types is a "map" that describes nine types of personalities, the main character traits, the relationship with the world, the propensities, as well as the evolutionary predispositions based on one's own strengths and areas. for improvement. It is something more than a mere classification, but a model that leads to a system in motion, a dynamic structure in which each enneatype encompasses the potential of all others, without being better or worse than others, but simply equally different and therefore unique: in the dynamics of the enneagram they are all rich in potential and, according to their evolution or involution, they tend towards a certain type of positivity or characteristic negativity.

The nine types of the enneagram are the following:

Type 1 - Perfectionist-Reformer

The Type One persons are conscientious and with a great innate ethical sense, with a great feeling of right and wrong. They are teachers, individuals who want to do something for others and change the world as promoters of change. Always fighting to improve things and at the same time fearful of making mistakes. Well organized, orderly and meticulous, they try to maintain high standards and can slip into being critical and perfectionist. Critics towards themselves and others, the Types One are people who aim to improve things inside and outside of themselves, creating a world of justice and moral order. They instinctively evaluate situations by judging what is good or bad, what is right or wrong. They are perfectionists, correct and sincere. They have practical meaning, self-control, seriousness and inflexibility. They can be pedantic and fussy.

- They establishes ideals of perfection that protects from external attacks; for this reason they tend to be intolerant and judgmental towards those who do not share them (he thinks he is always right).
- They tending towards perfection and avoids all that is imperfect: some emotions are judged negative and for this reason repressed (for example anger, anger, anger). To express the repressed emotional energy, they marry ideals for which to fight (it is a logical pretext for manifesting imperfect emotions). They love respect for the rules and wants others to observe them too.
- They have an image of himself as an honest person.
- The compulsion towards perfection pushes him to improve more and more.
- Long-term planning is preferred at the expense of short-term planning as it allows him to do "perfect things".

<u>Merits</u>

Correct and reliable
They carefully ponder the objectives
Respectful of the rules
sorted
Realists
Equipped with self-control

Defects

judging

Intolerant, impatient

Obsessive / Compulsive

Excessively logical

Anxious, they tend to somatize tensions

Type 2 - Selfless - Helper

Types Two are extremely empathic, sincere and kind-hearted individuals. They are friendly, generous and sacrifice themselves, but they can also be sentimental, flattering and complacent. They have good intentions and are motivated to be close to others, but they can slip into doing things for others in order to be considered necessary. This happens because they have an extreme need to serve and find in the cause of help and cooperation a true reason for living. They seek affection and approval. They want to be loved and appreciated, becoming indispensable to others. They have a spirit of sacrifice and are dedicated to others, but at the same time they tend to manipulate them. It is expansive and tends to give good advice. If he does not feel gratified, he can become whining and feel a victim. His behavior, aimed at satisfying the expectations of others, is generated by the fundamental need to feel loved.

- When it relates to others, they focus on seeking confirmation of affection.
- To receive these confirmations, they tend to seduce unconsciously.
- It could get to indirectly pleasing those who can express their wishes.

- When consociates someone tends to establish friendship immediately without thinking about possible deceptions.

Merits

Lovely

They take care of others

flexible

empathic

Excited

Defects

They tend to rely on guilt

Possessive

Manipulative

Excessively confident: they do not think of possible deceptions

Excessively conciliatory

They do not recognize their needs

Type 3 - Organizer - Realizer - Manager

The types Three are self-confident, attractive and fascinating. They are the classic people that when you meet them you can only look and estimate how they talk and move. Ambitious, competent and energetic, they can be worried about their social condition and strongly motivated to progress. They are diplomats and posed, but they may also be too worried about their image and what others think of them. They typically have problems with work addiction and competition. They try to be loved for their abilities and for what they do, sometimes neglecting themselves. These people have an extremely lively and reactive personality, are capable and efficient, and strongly wish to succeed in their lives. But often they live in a state of continuous confrontation and always give great importance to what appears. The risk he runs is to confuse the true self with the typical image of the group to which it belongs (double-breasted manager, super-mother).

- They love to be always on the move and not have "holes" during the day
- They tend to have a positive mentality as it projects a positive image to the outside
- Their compulsion is in wanting to achieve success at all costs: the word failure tends to frighten them. For this reason they only accept challenges where they know they can achieve the best possible result.
- They focus on goals by disengaging all kinds of negative thinking (convergent thinking)
- They suppress values to embody the social ones that can guarantee them recognition (traditionalist).
- Hyperactivity is the tool that allows them to stun his emotional part (they avoid questioning).

Merits

- Confident and extremely positive
- They love efficiency and practicality
- They tend to be excellent motivators
- Hyper-active

Defects

- They tend to mystify reality to project a positive image
- They tend to give the image a predominant role
- They are vindictive
- Merchant orientation

Type 4 - Romantic - Individualist - Artist

The four types are self-conscious, sensitive and reserved. These people are predisposed to embrace a positive emotion that leads them to become honest, creative and private individuals, but they can also be moody and hasty. They can feel a sense of vulnerability and deficiency that makes them hide from the world and a contempt for ordinary ways of living, to the point of feeling exempt from them. They have great artistic sense, a taste for beauty, a sense of color. They are intuitive, romantic, dreamers, extravagant. Melancholy and do not know how to live in the present: they take refuge in the past or dream about the future. They love the unusual, the eccentric, the exceptional. They express themselves through art: they can be poets, musicians, painters, designers. They do not disdain strange situations, scandals and forbidden things.

- The romantic is gifted with intuition: he has an excellent contact with his emotional part and does not yield to rationality.
- analytical and tend to go deep into situations
- They tend to be not very concrete in the sense that it is lacking in action because they love to reflect too long
- They tend to be considered authentic and different from the others
- They hate routine and love everything out of the ordinary

- In life they have constantly looking for situations full of emotional intensity, an element that makes them feel the life and the real people
- Integrated romantics have empathic abilities so high as to touch on telepathy: from a simple change in tone of voice they include the emotional alchemies of the interlocutor
- Its most obvious weak point is the tendency to idealize the future and not to act in the immediate present

Merits

- Introspective
- Creative / Artistic
- Equipped with great intuition
- Empaths
- They love emotional depth / able to renew themselves and transform their experiences

Defects

- Tend to melancholy
- Closed
- They tend to feel inadequate and self-pitying
- Lunatics
- They tend to live too much with their heads in the clouds

Type 5 - Thinker - Investigator - Observer

The Five types are sharp, intuitive, curious and are able to engage and focus on developing complex ideas and skills. They are independent, innovative and inventive, but they can also let themselves be absorbed by their imaginary thoughts and elaborations and become detached, while remaining hypersensitive and intense. They prefer to establish a profound autonomy in relationships with other people and generally act at a certain emotional distance from others. They defend their intimacy and don't get involved even in more relaxed situations that require social cooperation. They speak little, they are introverts and observers. Good listeners, quiet, but they also appear cold and distant.

- They tend to prefer observation rather than acting: they live in a mental world that is not real
- They read a lot and dream of omniscience. For them, knowledge is the element that motivates most of their actions. In fact, I firmly believe that knowing is power.
- They prefer distances in relationships and do not like too intrusive individuals, these people have a high sense of privacy and respect for personal intimacy.
- They tend to have a strong internal reference and use an impenetrable filter for reality only with rationality
- Despite being endowed with a strong intellectual power, they do not like to provide knowledge to others.

Merits

- They love the analysis of situations
- If integrated, they tend to be objective and omniscient
- They have good control over their emotions
- They create links between different disciplines / they are often pioneers, at the forefront in many things

Defects

- They believe they know more than others and think they are eccentric
- They tend to be stingy
- They are emotionally detached
- They tend to isolate themselves
- They tend to be critical of others
- They are Negative individuals

Type 6 - Loyal Skeptic - Collaborator

The Six types are reliable, faithful, responsible and hard workers. They are reference figures in every working context and in fact they are among those elements that manage to pursue and achieve great professional goals. They are very good at identifying problems, predicting them and encouraging cooperation, but they can become defensive, become evasive, anxious and go on with nerves complaining. One of their ambivalent aspects is their way of being too cautious and undecided, but also reactive and having a defiant and defiant attitude. They usually have problems with self-doubt and suspicion. Type Six is committed and safety oriented. He is fearful, conscientious, tormented by doubt. He is sometimes suspicious and suspicious. He is led to postpone and is afraid to act because exposing himself can lead to being attacked. It has team spirit, is reliable, faithful and faithful to the rules. He identifies with the causes of the weak, sacrifices himself and is faithful to the cause. The "counterphobic" type is extremist, provocative, reckless, risk-loving.

- Tends to be pessimistic and to see negative perspectives behind possible decisions

- His attention is focused on the possibility that something terrible may happen
- Analyzes the behavior of those around him as he is afraid of being manipulated or cheated
- In big decisions, he relies on someone he considers "authority". He is afraid to take them alone
- They are not people who easily trust
- Tends to be loyal to the authority represented by a head of work or even by the partner

Merits

- Wings
- instill courage and trust in themselves and others.
- Practical
- Inwardly stable and self-confident

Defects

- Anxious
- They can become paranoid
- They are wary
- They are excessively tied to the schemes
- Tend to procrastinate
- Ambivalents and with discontinuous emotional behavior

Type 7 - Optimistic - Hedonist

These people have the great power to always see the best of life and are often guided by a condition of vitality, joy and permanent energy that makes them attractive. He is an extrovert, creative and open to the opportunities that life offers. He has many interests, is communicative and versatile, loves to play and have fun. He loves variety and everything that helps to celebrate life: travel, parties, songs, restaurant meals. He wants to have "more" than everything and doesn't want to grow (a kind of joyful Peter Pan). He often has weight problems (he hates diets) and lives by excesses at all hours of the day and night, he does not care about the consequences and firmly thinks that it is better to enjoy the present in order not to live by regrets and probabilities.

- Tends to be hyperactive. If it is blocked by something it goes into crisis.
- It is constantly looking for different experiences.
- Love carefree
- It starts many things but only a few are finished
- "Freedom" is the engine of his actions

Merits

- Fun and joyful
- They tend to be spontaneous
- They love creativity
- They are extremely curious
- Dynamic

Defects

- They love to be the center of attention
- They tend to be impulsive and dispersive
- They don't like being limited in freedom (unruly)
- Suffer from restlessness

Type 8 - Chief - Strong - Decision-making

The Eight types are self-confident, strong and assertive. They are protective, resourceful, resolute and direct in speaking, but they can also be self-centered and dominant. Being close to these people often conveys a feeling of security because they tend to take control and say that everything will be fine thanks to their projects. They feel they need to control their environment, especially people, sometimes becoming controversial and intimidating. The Eight type is a strong, realistic and action-oriented person at work. He has clear and profound opinions on things. He has a strong sense of justice: protective and combative, he often defends himself and his loved ones. He is aggressive, direct, authoritarian, he gives orders willingly. It controls everything and everyone, and tends to impose its power on others. It is provocative, quarrelsome, quarrelsome, and can cause fear.

- Justice is lived in a subjective way
- Loves to control people and situations
- He is extremely and possessive (he defends his friends even if they are wrong)
- Loves fights based on loyalty and hates deception
- It does not tolerate being controlled
- Tents for leadership

Merits

- They tend to be direct
- They are authoritative
- They love loyalty
- They are protective

- They are safe themselves

Defects

- Tend to control others
- They tend to be rebellious if controlled
- They can become aggressive
- They cannot stand individuals who escape their range

Type 9 - Mediator - Diplomatic

The Nine types are welcoming, confident and balanced. They live in a positive dimension where everything happens for a certain reason and they don't believe in decisions made without pondering. They are usually creative, optimistic and capable of giving support, but may tend to be too compliant to keep the peace. They want everything to go smoothly and without conflict, but they tend to feel complacent, simplifying problems and minimizing anything that bothers them. They typically have problems with indolence and stubbornness. The Nine type is a calm, friendly and practical person, characterized by goodness, simplicity and natural kindness. They hate hasty judgments and those who despise their acquaintances. He is not inclined to criticize or judge people, but rather tries to bring reconciliation and peace back to where there is tension and conflict. He is diplomatic, sincere and loving. It is also quite influential, is carried away by the current and is ambivalent.

- Tend towards harmony and peace.
- To achieve these goals, they adapt to others (positive chameleon figure) avoiding contrasts

- They have concentration problems and do not know how to create a priority order during the day (important commitments are always postponed)
- They love programs and hate the unexpected

Merits

- Extremely available, indomitable and inclusive
- Peaceful
- Tolerances
- They can identify convergence points during arguments

Defects

- They tend to be absent during interactions
- Without concentration
- Passive-aggressive (they shut themselves up in silence when they are admitted to someone)
- They tend to always agree even if they are not
- Do not respect the commitments (irresponsible), simplify problems and minimize anything that bothers them

Knowing yourself is the only possibility you have if you want to grow, go beyond this deadlock you are feeling. You feel like you're ready to take off, but you don't know where you left your wings. With this book I will help you find them thanks to the ancient practice of the Enneagram. When you have finished reading if you think you finally have a tool to deal with your life, please leave a review on Amazon to let everyone know that this book has the answer to many problems that so many people have.

DON'T BE AFRAID TO KNOW YOURSELF

Knowing oneself is tiring and, in some cases, a little painful, but only in this way can we take the reins of our lives. Did you ever look at yourself in the mirror and not understand who the hell was that person reflected? If you often do not know why you have reached the point where you are, if you do not understand the decisions you have made, if you think your stupidity is something intolerable know that you are not stupid, you are just an individual who needs to better understand their own personality, accept it and live according to a regime of high honesty. Get rid of all the buildings, find your spaces and live free to breathe in a better world.

What do you see when you look at yourself in the mirror? Are you happy with what you see, not just on a physical level, or would you like to be a completely different person? Are you aware of how you are?

What does it mean to know yourself?

It means knowing how to stop, despite the hectic pace of everyday life, and learn to listen to each other, to read the intricacies of one's soul, the one who knows who we are, the one who hides our desires, the one who can indicate the path to follow. Soul, psyche, heart, no matter what the name you attribute to the core nucleus that characterizes you, as long as you can stop and make intimate knowledge of it. Sometimes we believe we know each other, but what we see is only a reflection of what others think and say about us. If this is perfectly normal in childhood, in adulthood it is necessary to come to terms with what we really are, looking at what is really hidden within us or we will risk acting to please others, giving them our lives.

The compelling need to change can be hidden in a tiring moment, when things do not turn, when we feel paralyzed. This is the occasion to look inside oneself, avoiding to escape introspection, throwing oneself on other activities or running aground following the advice of others, imitating their choices. Take in hand, start a deep friendship with yourself, give yourself time to deepen your knowledge of your core group, a strenuous and, in some cases, painful operation, but only in this way can we take over the reins of our lives and take paths evolutionary.

You have to know that when something goes wrong, most of us ask the wrong question ("why"), while the question that helps us take a step forward is "what?".

Instead of asking "why am I not happy at work?", Let's try to ask "what can I do to be?" In this way, we will be able not only to discover more about ourselves but also to know our capabilities.

Getting to know yourself better means having real benefits in return. What are the main ones? We list them below:

1. to know with more certainty what we want;
2. to have greater decision-making power;
3. to have the chance to be more creative;
4. being able to identify more easily the causes of our malaise;
5. to improve our self-esteem;
6. to improve the quality of our social and personal relationships.

"If you know the enemy and yourself, your victory is certain. If you know yourself but not the enemy, your chances of winning and losing

are equal. If you do not know the enemy or even yourself, you will succumb in every battle », Sun Tzu.

Knowing oneself is the ability to investigate within oneself, to discover and understand that the essence of our life is inside, not outside of us. The great Greek philosopher Socrates has made the "know thyself" a pivotal point of his thought, indeed of the entire ancient Greece, for the good of man, so that he may become what his deepest nature demands. If we stop to reflect, to meditate, to observe ourselves, we will be able to come to discover who we are, for which it is precisely the knowledge that allows man to know himself and therefore to know what is the most suitable way to live happily.

iWe can dare to say that the Greek sages have introduced the I into the western world and for the first time man coincides with his interiority, with his soul. But what does it mean to know oneself today, in the modern age? Knowing oneself first of all means knowing one's limits, because it is unthinkable to reach happiness if we do not accept ourselves as we are. This does not mean that we have to fossilize ourselves, but it is a fundamental starting point for embarking on an evolutionary path, of spiritual awakening, because it is precisely starting from the awareness of limits, that we can overcome them and improve ourselves. Once we have acquired this awareness, everyone can take care of what belongs to him, to do what he does best. One must follow one's vocations in order to enhance one's abilities and put them at the service of others. A just society based on "know yourself" should allow people to do what they were born for. Vocational work is the only way that allows the individual to do his work with love and passion, whatever it is.

And it is at this point that knowing oneself becomes a source of happiness, as a means to reach self-knowledge, and to travel the only path that leads to happiness. All it takes is a good dose of courage to look reality in the face and tell yourself the truth. In today's society, unfortunately, we hide too often behind ourselves because it is easier to appear than to be, and it is the same society that does not want us to be ourselves. In reality most of us are not interested at all in knowing each other, deluded as it is to already know everything. And it is in this illusion that at some point in our lives, the lack of knowing oneself leads to a total sense of loss, because we will no longer know who we really are, where we are and what we are doing here. And no external response can come to our aid.

This lack of inner security will essentially be due to an almost total unawareness of who we really are: it is as if our interaction with ourselves, with others, with our work, with our normal activities, produces only dissonances and inner voids . We feel immersed in a reality that does not belong to us, unsure of our choices and decisions, uncertain about the way forward, and we no longer know who we are and what we really want. All this causes unhappiness!

We all feel if we are good or bad, if we perceive feelings of lightness or heaviness, well-being or discomfort. The area of intimate feeling should become the place of analysis, observation, taking charge of what should be eliminated, elaborated, expanded, integrated or transformed on the basis of what is necessary to carry out in order to promote fullness expression of their own requests for fulfillment.

Human beings are not born with destructive but creative tendencies. He wishes to manifest his inner nature, as an acorn wants to become the tree that it is.

Each person is unique, since each person has a genetic datum that distinguishes him and subjective experiences that have marked him on the basis of emotional and affective imprints, both negative and positive. There is no doubt that two children (even twins) who grew up in the same family present different temperamental traits and establish completely different relational dynamics with their parents and social environment. The deepest aspiration deposited in the human being is that of manifesting one's existence, through a vision and a mission that give meaning and meaning to the fact of having come into the world. Human beings are not born with destructive but creative tendencies. He wishes to manifest his inner nature, as an acorn wants to become the tree that it is. No human being loves infidelity to his own nature, although he can betray himself and his vocation.

When this happens a profound sensation of anguish and existential emptiness arises. To become the tree that we are we need a favorable environment, where we can manifest the light of authenticity that is already present in us and which must not be purchased anywhere. When this process of revelation of one's true self is interrupted or castrated, we assume that there are disharmonies of behavior that can lead to psychosomatic manifestations, neuroses of various kinds and, in the most serious cases, psychotic states. When we decide to restore order in our disorder and take the path of homecoming, every form of discomfort begins to be cured, behaviors correct and a feeling of peace and harmony is released that grows with the passing of the healing process.

All this requires a serious commitment to work with the utmost honesty on oneself, not being afraid to meet one's inner monsters or drowning in puddles of pain frozen in the depths of forgetfulness. The fact of being able to grow does not cancel the fragility of which we are composed or the limits of which we are constituted but it integrates them with the possibilities of finding solutions, of reworking a wound, of activating new resources in order to become more and more human and to find the beauty inside and outside us in a face illuminated by faith and love for oneself, for others and for the Absolute. All this is not possible unless we understand that our decisions are what guide us towards maturity, in the lightness of a soul that makes somersaults of happiness within the sky of possibilities. The truth is that knowing yourself helps us to live better.

Try to understand why you lie and to whom. We have all told a few lies, to other people and to ourselves, and for different reasons. Developing a systematic plan to be more honest, however, will be difficult if you fail to identify these reasons and the people you lie to most often.

- The lies to make a good impression include hyperboles, embellishments and inventions that we tell others, and ourselves, to make us feel better about our inadequacies. When you are unhappy for some reason, it is much easier to fill the void with lies than to tell the truth.
- We tell lies to our peers that we consider better than us because we want their respect. Unfortunately, being dishonest is a lack of respect in the long run. Recognize people the ability to understand you at a deeper level.
- The lies that prevent us from being embarrassed' include the lies told to hide improper behavior, transgressions or activities we are not proud of. If your mother found a pack of cigarettes in your jacket, you could lie and say that I belong to a friend of yours to avoid punishment.

- We tell lies to the authority figures to avoid embarrassment and punishment. When we have done something for which we feel guilty, we tell lies to eliminate guilt and avoid punishment.

Now I want to give you a small gift to really begin to understand that knowing yourself and living according to a universal law of honesty is the best thing you can do.

Below you will find two easy exercises to do for your personal growth path. They are part of the great and wise practice of the Enneagram and allow you to have a better awareness of your whole being. Don't be afraid to start getting to know yourself, immediately start the road to your happy future.

EXERCISE # 1 - Learn the sound of your voice

It sounds crazy but none of us initially has the true knowledge of our own voice. And the voice says everything about a person, it is the most powerful tool with which humans establish a bridge with other people. Learning the sound, accepting every nuance of the tone of your voice is the first big step towards a conscious life. Take a book, a book you know very well and read aloud with a voice recorder (the one on your smartphone will do just fine) three pages every day for a week. Record your voice in the morning and then listen again in the evening. Learn to understand your tones and your vibrations.

EXERCISE # 2 - Do not lie

Even adult people are in a position to tell small lies. Even simply to look more interesting. A little tale told to the neighbor to impress him with fantastic holidays, a lie without malice so as not to make a grandmother worry. Here in this exercise I want to ask you to choose two hours a day when you don't tell lies. No lie of any kind, always and only to the truth.

To be honest with yourself is to be consistent with your thinking and acting. Sometimes it is very difficult to keep ourselves consistent, but if we succeed it means that we really know each other, we accept each other and we are satisfied with us. If this were not the case, if we lied to ourselves, how could we expect others to be sincere towards us? Whoever is not honest with himself has a strong desire to be what he is not and only by taking refuge in lies does he feel fulfilled.

Nobody likes lies. Unfortunately, being dishonest with others and ourselves is in some cases simpler than telling the truth. But it doesn't have to be this way: learning to be honest and not feeling the need to lie can help you improve your relationships and lighten your conscience. Slightly changing your perspective and choosing an honesty policy can help you not need to lie and let you tell the truth more willingly.

LIFE IS FULL OF CYCLICAL TEMPORAL TRAPS

Now the time has come to think about the time and its way of arriving in cycles of events that are repeated and that we must be able to manage. time understood as personal, experiential time; history as a life story, events and teachings drawn from everyday life, behaviors borrowed from others, learned and reinterpreted in the light of their own canons, their education, their morals and their social sentiment. History of life, therefore, but with the clear I intend to reveal those "courses and appeals" that mark the moments; those gestures, those situations, those emotions that we often find ourselves emphasizing with the exclamation "Here, it happened again!". Life traps "or lifetraps, real ways of thinking, feeling, acting and relating that have been formed in fundamental moments of development and that over time have been structured into real traps. People often do not recognize them simply by identifying them with "destiny", thus surrendering to the possibility of changing their lives and subverting the patterns that determine them. However, some may recognize the dysfunction of the cage and choose to avoid the "active trigger" situation, or they tend to overcompensate with behaviors that are clearly opposed to those that actually belong to the scheme. What nevertheless appears clear, however, is that these cages do not allow for satisfactory and happy social relations because the people who are imprisoned do not really know either themselves or others. The schemes, in fact, are formed on the occasion of early experiences when the needs of the child have not been adequately interpreted by the caregiver, or by the figure of occurrence. The child has thus had to play force to hide his true Self and its emotional world, in favor of one more acceptable to the other which thus guarantees him closeness and care. It is therefore a matter of early maladaptive patterns, that is organizations of the experience according to distorted relational, behavioral, cognitive and affective patterns and fruit of the "sick" encounter between the child's temperament and his experiences with the caregiver.

We therefore understood how these patterns are formed, but what causes them to continue to operate? What keeps them active?

Since these traps are a way of reading and living the others and the world, in a pervasive and stable way, over time they are the most reliable compass for orienting oneself in relationships and with oneself. It is self-evident that this is a known, familiar and therefore "comfortable" and reassuring solution for the person when he finds himself answering questions such as "How are the others?" "What do I want?" does it move in the world? ". The trap thus becomes part of itself, a part that blends with its own Self and that clearly tells us who we are, who the others are and how we move around the world and, the most devastating thing is that, precisely because of the their "presumed truthfulness", we cling desperately, even paying the high price of pain.

So what are these traps?

Abandonment: we are convinced that we lose the people we love (by death or because we leave each other) and to be alone "Please don't leave me!"

Distrust and abuse: the abused person (abuse means any violation of personal, mental and physical boundaries) is constantly on guard. "I do not trust you!"

Emotional deprivation: the person experiences a real affective desert: loneliness and detachment, combined with a sense of emptiness and frustration of their own needs. "I will never have the love I need"

Social exclusion: one feels alone, isolated, excluded, unwanted and different with a consequent high state of anxiety.

Dependency: one has the feeling of not being able to do it alone, of not knowing how to look after oneself, therefore one needs constantly the help of others.

Vulnerability: you feel vulnerable, anything can happen at any time and you do not have the resources to face the situation with a consequent peak of anxiety.

Inadequacy: we feel something wrong inside, we don't feel adequate or worthy of love and we do everything to keep this hidden, with relative shame when instead this belief emerges. "I am not worth anything!"

Bankruptcy: we are considered to be bankrupt compared to others and, if good results are achieved, we feel like impostors, we think we do not deserve it.

Submission: one feels dominated by those around us; welcomes the other and is satisfied unconditionally. Passivity becomes a tool to get back a good self-image.

Strict standards: we must always do more and do better. One must be the best in everything one does, without ever stopping, without ever relaxing, with its anxious state that emerges if these standards have not been reached.

Claim: the others "owe" you respect, love, closeness and if this does not occur, you feel anger because you consider yourself a victim and feel frustrated.

Once the trap and its recursion have been identified in particular situations or with specific types of people, all that remains is to act and subvert the scheme.

Such as? Referring to small tips, useful for pursuing the path of personal fulfillment:

- we awaken our "real" part which has been buried by years of submission, neglect, impositions, etc.; we listen to what he needs
- we express our needs and realize our desires: very often we did not do this because we could not or did not think we deserved it; now instead dedicate yourself some time and above all think about deserving it
- begin to enter into the perspective of possible change; if we want we can change, even if this will involve enormous effort
- we become aware of our traps and try to implement a change with an intent that is constant over time. Obviously this implies leaving the known and the familiar to explore unknown personal and relational territories, but if we do not throw ourselves "in the fray" the change cannot take place by itself. Support our help
- We begin to deal with situations and conditions that hurt us: it would be easier to implement those patterns that have anesthetized us for years, but if we really want to live with a new skin, we should not use shortcuts, but rather "try"; just so we will discover what we really are and want

Let's create a personal vision, or what we want and who we want to be. Ask yourself what really makes you happy, what makes you unique, what you really enjoy doing and above all consider yourself the only judge of yourself. Only you know what is good and what is detrimental to your person and, of course, respecting the rights of others, you begin to cultivate a healthy selfishness that allows you to speak in first person without feeling guilty or afraid of being judged.

Can the Enneagram help us achieve the one true purpose of everyone, that is, live happily?

If we exclude the mystical and esoteric uses, where this methodology of study of the personality has often found application, we will discover an effective system to understand who we are, how we relate to others and how to overcome our limits, in order to be happy.

Before understanding how to use this methodological approach to the study of personality, it is worth understanding why we should waste time informing ourselves about it. We have seen that the Enneagram substantially "classifies" people, consequently, if we know well the characteristics of each type, we can first of all understand ourselves, and secondly better understand others; since every enneatype brings strengths and weaknesses, being able to frame who we face, gives us the possibility to know him better, to know about things he has not told us (and maybe he doesn't want to tell us) and therefore to relate in as harmonious as possible.

At the same time we will discover how we are really made, that is what our weaknesses and abilities are, and therefore where we have to work to become better individuals and what to focus on to achieve the results we want.

It goes without saying that, knowing ourselves better and others, we will be able to weave better, deeper and more sincere relationships, in order to live better, because, I am profoundly convinced of it, true happiness in life is achieved by spending all of it the energies in the relationship with others, and giving very little importance to work and money.

The study of the Enneagram, however, has an even more interesting purpose than to improve oneself in relation to oneself and to others; the deepest secret is to use it to overcome one's limitations and obtain a truer and more complete world view. Most of our behaviors derive from well-established habits, patterns that we tend to repeat, for an unconscious fear of changing the status quo, breaking the balance in which we live and running into problems that we don't want. In reality this fear (we have talked about it at length) is unjustified and prevents people from changing, solving their problems, turning around the situation in which we find ourselves and emancipating ourselves.

The Enneagram helps us in this, to see things from a new point of view, through the correct interpretation of our behavior and that of others; in a sense it can be considered as a window on a new world.

At this point we try to understand how to exploit this powerful tool to "live better"; Let's take a look at the graphic representation of the Enneagram, a sort of nine-pointed star, enclosed within a circle.

THE JAPANESE RESTAURANT STORY

Self-esteem and self-confidence determine personal and professional fulfillment. It is the key to accessing your goals. The lack of self-confidence translates into a devaluation of the person: phrases like "I am worthless", "I am not able", "I have no quality" are on the agenda in the inner dictionary of those who lack self-esteem. Those who lack confidence in themselves often struggle to draw up a list of their qualities.

Now I want to tell you to do something, something that may seem silly but instead it is a very useful exercise to understand and get on with your life. Go to the bathroom and look at yourself in the mirror, look at your reflection and think about who you are and who you've been all these years. Speak your name out loud now. "I am Adam Night and I am a wonderful person". "Adam Night". Repeat your name over and over until the sound of it sounds familiar. Once again.

You did it?

Well.

Now take a sheet of paper and write ten qualities of yourself. This exercise is very effective. Add to the list everything that comes to you from others like compliments for example, especially those that you don't regularly recognize and accept. Often when self-confidence is lacking, one feels responsible for failures and never for successes. What you do is your responsibility! So if you make a mistake the responsibility is yours, in the same way if you succeed the credit is all yours. Remember that our brain is more sensitive to negative events: we remember more a criticism than five compliments received. This is why it is absolutely necessary to have a positive dialogue with oneself that allows you to direct thoughts about successes and not about failures, resources and not constraints.

Being aware of your qualities is essential to encourage and nurture self-esteem, but to grow and improve as people and professionals, you need to be aware of your areas of development. You have to question yourself and work on what you can improve: your flaws.

Here is another important exercise for you: take a sheet and write a list of your defects.

This exercise will probably be easier than the previous one. Once you have compiled the list of defects, take one and decide to improve it. Daily constancy and frequency are important. Do you always have negative thoughts? Try for 30 days to replace negative thoughts with positive messages. If it is not enough 30 days extended until the target is reached and go to the next defect. If you really commit yourself, you can get rid of 6 defects in a year. The aim is not to achieve perfection, but to improve and increase your personal value.

Remember that being aware of your defects also means knowing how to accept them and avoid putting yourself in difficult situations.

Now I want to ask you something: can you say thank you?

Say it three times in a loud voice.

Learn to accept compliments, don't refuse them, but answer THANK YOU. If the feedback does not come spontaneously then ask for it "how did I feel during my conference speech?", "I was effective?"

If you answer negatively you will know what to improve, if you receive a compliment it will be sugar for your self-esteem.

Maybe not everyone knows it but learning to compliment is really essential to have a greater self-awareness because it allows you to have a better relationship with compliments, whatever they are. In fact the first step to receive them is to make them.

Making compliments means being attentive to people, observing them and this is very pleasing.

Now I tell you what you will do to improve this aspect of yourself, during this week in a sincere and authentic way you make a compliment following a good deed that you intend to reinforce.

At first it may seem like a stretch, but as you compliment it it will come naturally to you and you will become a distributor of natural smiles.

I just have to ask you to have the maximum honesty in this exercise, you have to always and only tell the truth and don't give compliments if they are not sincere and authentic because in this case the lies would have the exact opposite effect and they would distance you from your final resolution goal and awareness of your inner person.

I want to tell you a story. And it's a story that really happened when I was twenty-four and I lived in Seattle. I had just graduated and was looking for a job. I was a smart boy, I had few good friends but in college I was one of those who studied diligently but never exaggerated. I liked going out with friends but I didn't particularly love parties. We went to eat a pizza and watch a movie at the cinema, sometimes I took a girl out for a date. I was a quiet boy with a normal life. I had my ambitions, but they were still submerged by life and youth. One day I was with two friends of mine in a new downtown Japanese restaurant. It was a very elegant place, with precious antique vases in the hall, wonderful prints on the wall and an atmosphere that exuded opulence. Before that I had been eating sushi in some place near the college, but no place was like that. When I crossed the threshold of that Japanese restaurant I felt with a one-way ticket for the inconvenience, I was entering a place that I wasn't completely familiar with and where I was finding too many details of unease. The waiters were dressed in elegant suits and spoke slowly with a fake smile on their faces. They looked at me and watched my clothing. Maybe they thought I was too young for a place like that. Maybe they thought my jeans and my unbranded shirt were not the most appropriate attire for their restaurant. It was called "Empire of the Sun: Japanese Restaurant". The name already expressed the whole concept of those precious vases and those prints on the wall. My friend Tom had come to my house that afternoon and asked me if I wanted to go and try that new restaurant, I said yes without enthusiasm I didn't like changing habits and for me the Japanese restaurant was only one until then. His name was Yoshi and was frequented by all the college kids. We liked it because it was cheap and Seattle's prettiest girls went there too. And then after dinner the waiter came and offered you a small bottle of cold sake to digest. It was perfect. But that night we weren't there, my friends and I were in this new restaurant and I was going to figure out one of the greatest lessons of my life.

My friends and I looked at each other for a moment, then we all looked at the waiter and overcoming the sense of annoyance and discomfort we all felt we entered and followed him to our table. We had arrived there and none of us would have ever had the courage to say "let's go this place is not for us". We sat down, we looked at each other with a hesitant look but now we were there. The table was elegantly set with precious ceramic bowls. A waitress gives me the menu, I take it and open it. The various dishes were written in Japanese and the prices were exorbitant. That dinner would have cost me half of what I had on my bank account. I was sure every dish would be delicious, but I was not such a keen Japanese cooking enthusiast that I wanted to spend all that money on a dinner. I could not. I was young and I had a precarious job, I still had to realize myself. I don't call myself a stingy person, but I am a man who has always valued money. This is my being. This is my way of life. It's part of me. I felt the weight of what was happening on my shoulders and I absolutely didn't want to be at that moment. But what could I do? Here then is that at that moment my head, my mind made a mental click. There was a real leap. I realized that I absolutely must not deny myself and my way of seeing the world. I must always give priority to my feeling. Always. So I looked at my friends and simply told them what I thought, we left. Probably the waiter thought we were poor, but the moral of this whole story is that I don't care at all about what other people think. Or rather, I care because I am not a self-centered person who thinks only of himself but I understand that the decisions I make must be decisions that make me feel good and that do not obscure everything that I am. And this happens both in big decisions like buying a house or changing jobs, and in smaller decisions like deciding to get up from the table because menu prices are too expensive. This is great advice, I give you this rule of life, never underestimate its importance.

When you want to get up from the table, any table, do it and follow your instincts.

I just named the word instinct. What does it mean?

We often name it but it is not always clear what it really means. Acting by instinct, seeking a flow of actions without being held back by the structures that a person can build when he thinks too much and does not follow his own desires.

The word instinct indicates an action or behavior performed by an animal or a person automatically, without being aware of it, due to an internal force within the organism.

The definition of instinct, in this sense, also extends to purely psychic and mental actions, such as, for example, the same cognitive activity, which can be considered as a natural instinct, unlike those psychic processes that are based on patterns I learned.

According to the psychology of common sense, animal behavior is essentially based on instincts, which allow the survival of individual animals and their species through the satisfaction of the primary needs of hunger, thirst, sleep and sex. Human behavior, on the other hand, would be only minimally instinctive, because even actions aimed at satisfying primary needs would be guided by conscience and shaped by social and cultural factors.

The theme of instinct is strongly connected with the practice of the Enneagram and it is not possible to understand the whole structure of this ancient knowledge without understanding in depth the theme of instinct and the various types of first-born strength that push us to commit a certain action . When a person does not know this subject and studies only the "nine types" he inevitably makes important mistakes in identifying his own personality or the personality of other people, thus unjustly attributing characteristics to the nine profiles and running the risk of stereotyping. But there is another even more relevant reason: only those who explore the theme of instincts are able to open an important front of inner work, with themes that are responsible for some of the most rooted and "neurotic" aspects of our personalities.

Instincts concern survival strategies that all animals (even animals that are not mammals) adopt, in different areas. Although there are different types of instincts - such as maternal, masculine or feminine, for example - in the Enneagram we study three specific types of instincts: the conservative (also known as self-conservative), the social and the sexual. All these instincts belong to what is conventionally called the instinctive center in the contemporary movement of the Enneagram, linked to the most visceral, automatic, rapid and unconscious sensations and reactions we have; reactions that are mainly commanded by our primitive brain, also called reptilian brain.

Some things are non-negotiable, that is, they must happen. Thus, the behaviors deriving from the instinctive field are part of our level of being, that "animal soul" which comes to dominate in some situations or which remains latent in others. The important thing is therefore to be able to arrive at a more opportune possibility of equilibrium. These behaviors come from a level of being lower than the human level and still much more distant from the level of being more directly linked to Essence, which is the most evolved part of each of us. Instincts are related to a part of us that is inferior to our personality and that can be called a false personality.

If our personality, as shown by the Enneagram through the lower emotional and mental center, shows us our passions and fixations, we must understand that this is already a great distortion of what we really are, instincts are still a level distortion inferior that they form a mask on our existence, and therefore represent a distortion of our own personality.

When the functioning of instincts is healthy, instincts come into action in a manner pertinent to a given situation and always to the right extent. In this case the instincts do not take care of such a significant part of our life experience and leave room for the most refined centers of intelligence.

In the healthy use of one's instincts, for example, the self-conservative instinct is the one that fortunately comes into action to protect us when our physical survival begins to be truly threatened - for example in times of financial crisis, when we are hungry or sleepy , during a very cold climate, or during a robbery.

To increase confidence in yourself, you have to get out of the established patterns, with reassuring habits. Pay attention to everything you do every day because the principle to remember is one step at a time, gently, without revolutions.

Make a list of small challenges! From the most "easy" to the most "difficult" for you. Start with the first challenge. Until it is won, don't go to the next one!

No pressure, if it takes you two months it's not serious. The goal is simply to move, change habits.

The social instinct is the one that comes into action to help us produce, among other things, the very important experiences of belonging, of collaborating and connecting - and in healthy use it tends to come into action only at times when these things are more at risk or when they are desirable.

The sexual instinct, on the other hand, is activated to allow us to create closer ties with other individuals, by means of a true union and communion, through the experiences of connection with vital energy, like the whole - and, once again, it tends to go into action only when these constraints begin to falter or when they have to increase a little.

Instincts also hide both deeper shadows and characteristics related to spiritual functions and the higher nature of the human being. They also hide, in my opinion, some secrets of what I call our soul schema, and of specific spiritual lineages. In the following articles I will briefly discuss some of these aspects.

However, unfortunately, the general state of the human being is very limited due to a much diminished conscience. Therefore, the vast majority of people experience strong distortions in the use of instincts, due to unresolved traumas and complexes, which, unconsciously, make us lose the due energy balance in relation to instincts. Instincts become more active and begin to command our daily experience of living, so as to overlap with our emotions and our thoughts, greatly limiting the quality of our existence. More specifically, each instinct distorts so as to operate above or below the appropriate level, all those times we perceive a feeling of threat in that specific sphere of life. All this usually happens at a profoundly unconscious level, but it must be unmasked by people engaged with their own self-development.

In summary there are two ways in which these distortions arrive:

1. The first mode occurs when we experience (usually unreal) threats to the sphere of life corresponding to a specific instinct and, as a reaction, we make sure that this instinct functions above its normal and desirable level, that is, when we unconsciously pass to the attempt to compensate for that feeling of scarcity or risk with a level in excess of that instinctive function.

2. The second mode occurs when the threats we perceive (these too usually unreal), linked to a specific instinct, ensure that an

opposite strategy is developed: that of reducing the level of functioning of that instinctive energy, which will then become insufficient and underused.

The third instinct tends to be more balanced, or to have some of the first or second strategy. Therefore it is the only one that tends to use closer to reality.

Depending on the specific distortion made by the person, behaviors, profiles and potentially very different problems arise between them. This happens at such a point that we can say that every order of instinct carries typical traces of people. In other words, the order of instincts generates a second typology within the Enneagram system, parallel to the most known typology, that of the Nine Types. Indeed, individuals with the same dominant and repressed instinct can often feel more similar to each other than individuals of the same enneatype who have different instinctive profiles. In the subject of relationships, for example, the instinctive profile is more relevant than the classic one, of the nine Enneagrams. And if sometimes the instinctive profile of an individual can be added to the profile of its enneatype, in some cases it can even contrast with some typical features expected.

KNOW YOUR INSTINCTS TO BE APPRECIATED BY OTHERS

Now the time has come to discover a great truth that does not always come out of people's lives.

Self-conscious people give importance to the right things and do not get lost in insignificant moments of their lives.

All those who work seriously and constantly on themselves have a knowledge of the mechanisms of their own personality that allows them to have greater confidence in themselves, a confidence that comes from within and not from outside - or if we prefer - which comes from a place that is true and not illusory.

Therefore they do not lose themselves in futile things, they do not try to make you feel inferior or attack you where you are weakest. They do not feel threatened or jealous. They know their limits and do not hide them.

Self-awareness is the basis of all those qualities that we aspire to see in the people we love most, the partner, children, parents and our friends. You know who you are and trust that the other person knows himself. Being kind becomes easier because we understand and make the other's emotions our own. This is empathy. Since you spend time processing your emotions you will also be more emotionally available and instead of feeling threatened, misunderstood and closed, you will be able to dedicate yourself to more authentic and sincere relationships.

The key to understanding the other person (children, parents, brothers, etc.) and connecting with it with renewed clarity lies within ourselves. After all, who wouldn't want a sincere partner? Well this will be your next "golden rule" for when you look for one - make sure you're the sincere partner.

Self-conscious people are nicer. In fact it is quite obvious if you think about your direct experiences or your knowledge that a self-aware companion or companion can become a real blast because they understand what makes living fun. They can be self-ironic and capable of making fun of themselves, not because they are insecure but because they understand their own gaps and limitations and are willing to put them out in the open instead of creating a false image of self-confident people.

A self-conscious person is a person who knows the right value of sincerity and will not lie to you. He will not tell you a comfortable lie in order not to "hurt your feelings." In an intimate relationship we need our counterpart to tell us things frankly. If we can't trust in intimate relationships what can we trust in the end? Conscious people are clear about their intentions and what they want. After seeing the painful effects that lies and dishonesty create in a relationship, you immediately recognize that the wisest thing to do is to refuse to create further garbage. Self-awareness can come out as something grumpy or too abrupt, but it's true - and what's real is always the best thing.

In today's world we live in a wrong dimension of empathy and only those who internalize the emotions of others can understand the pain and suffering that exists in the world. A self-conscious person is aware of what is around her at such a point that empathy goes to a higher level. People thus create better friendships and bonds because they respect and wonder at the human experience of each one. All this creates a sense of meaning and connection that most people do not have.

Now let's talk about self-preservation. It is a word that includes a wonderful ancestral concept: man has an intimate power, a force within himself that leads him on a path of protection against dangers. It is a tendency that oscillates between the very strong desire not to change a situation in which man's life is protected and a dimension of eternal search for new perspectives to get better and go into a better situation for himself and his family.

All people have something to protect and they want to protect themselves from external forces. In the moment in which certain actions are put in place to feel in a refuge far from the dangers of the world and of life, then it is the moment in which the instinct of self-preservation presents itself in all its wonderful ancestral ability.

The person who preserves himself adequately proves to be grateful for the enormous gift of life and is also responsible for treating him well and in a respectful way, as animals do, even those with simpler cell structures.

Preserving one's life and respecting other life forms is, after all, one of the most basic attitudes expected of all living beings. Among animals, in Nature, one kills only for one's own survival and preserves life in the most diverse ways, avoiding predators.

Furthermore, considering the level closest to the true entity of a human being and its healthier functioning, the self-conservative instinct is linked to the contemplative capacity and the most profound contact with silence. Another interesting element is the realization that it is very important to engage the body in the processes of development of consciousness.

Being "present" is the basis of the practice of those who invest in spiritual development, starting with the ability to feel totally connected to the body.

However, those who are exaggerated - the dominant self-preservatives - carry with them, if possible, a shadow of lack of confidence in life, thus defining a sort of attitude of greater distrust before destiny.

On the other hand, those who are insufficiently preserved - repressed self-preservatives - can have a similar shadow of mistrust on the fact that there is no one who provides what is necessary and does not help to adequately preserve life.

Both profiles often bring with them central traumas of episodes in which life has been threatened. Some examples of common traumas seen during the most profound workshops with the Enneagram are: physical, health or survival risks perceived during childhood or in the intrauterine period; ancient situations of lack of resources or deprivation; memories of systemic or even collective family pains related to hunger, death by war and scarcity.

The self-conservative instinct is obviously connected to the world of the mother who protects her children, the lioness who keeps her puppies safe, the mother who hugs and nurses children. The mother has the archetypal function of protecting the offspring and at the tribal level she preserves and protects life, the heirs of the social group and therefore the possibility of a specific whole social group to move forward into the future and establish a connection between present and future. Working on the relationship with the mother to resolve any trauma of this relationship is, for various reasons, indispensable for all those who place themselves on the path of self-development.

Sometimes it happens that the issues related to the mother tend to be perceived by the individual as more traumatic when the self-conservative instinct is dominant. Often there are cases in which individuals feel an addiction and an excessive attachment to the maternal figure compared to when the self-conservative instinct is repressed, where a probable excessive detachment from the maternal figure is generated.

The almost permanent, conscious or unconscious feeling of people who are dominant self-conservative is one in which life is threatened and something risky for survival can happen at any time. In practice, this feeling leads this group of people to have a more anxious, wary, risk-averse and pragmatic trait compared to other people of the same type as the Enneagram.

Quality of organization, punctuality and regularity are also common in dominant self-preservatives. People like this also tend to worry at least a little more with their health and with financial issues and controls. These people also tend to pay more attention to themselves and their priorities, compared to colleagues of the same type. As a side effect, I am at greater risk of being individualistic and having a shadow of egoism or even opportunism. The style tends to be more self-sufficient and introverted - however, always taking as a reference, in this comparison, the other colleagues of the same type.

Those who are repressed self-preservatives may have a tendency not to consider their lives as sufficiently important and, therefore, the subject of well-deserved care. With this, these people can demonstrate, in a voluntary or involuntary (active or passive) way, a certain negligence and even a contempt for life - mainly towards everyday life. On the other hand, there is a profile of audacity, risk appetite and a possible courageous entrepreneur attitude (while a dominant self-conservative can have more the profile of the manager rather than the entrepreneur).

Distraction, disorganization and aversion to routine can easily become weaknesses for these people, as well as a certain lack of attention to health issues and an obedience to the needs of the body. When compared to colleagues of the same type as the Enneagram, these people tend to be more extroverted.

Here is an exercise for you. I want you to think about your instincts to help you be more aware of yourself and all that surrounds you without the prejudices of the superstructures in which we live.

Premise for the success of the exercise: always look for honesty with yourself. Don't lie, it's useless. Lies are useless and take you away from your goal of a peaceful future.

Exercise: Take a notebook, choose a nice notebook that you like because it will become a small companion of adventures every day. Every day you write the date and write the things you did accompanying them by the instinct that guided your actions according to you. Put an asterisk next to the actions you could have done better and that you could have lived with a better mood.

HOW TO USE THE ENNEAGRAM

So far you've read a lot of things, but I'm sure you're still wondering: how can I use all this information to improve my life and become aware of myself?

Now I'll explain everything to you. As you already know, there are 9 fundamental types, and we all belong to only one of them. They are numbered from 1 to 9, and after 9 it resumes 1. However, it is not so easy, otherwise there would be only 9 personalities in all, and we know that it is not true.

However, there are "ALI". This term means the neighboring numbers, the previous and the following. For example, a type 1 will have wings in 9 and 2. They make sure they already have 18 types (two wings for each). Added to this are the levels. In fact, each type has 3 levels, depending on the level of development. And we are therefore 54 types (3 for each of the 18). Finally, the types are not fixed for life, but oscillate according to precise directions. Each type has 2 directions.

But every person lives a life of his own that includes different situations and experiences with different nuances of behavior due to what he has seen, done, learned over the course of his life. Ultimately, there are no two perfectly equal types.

The enneagram is not a system to frame a man or a woman in a predefined scheme but it serves to better know all that you are and have been. But that's not all: this is also an excellent way to better understand

and define other people and therefore to build long-lasting relationships that bring values and well-being to you too.

Let's start with the symbol of the Enneagram first. It summarizes each type and how the various types are related to one another. The various lines you see are not by chance, but indicate very specific routes. Maybe right now you're confused, but wait now I'll explain you better. Look carefully at the illustration I put below.

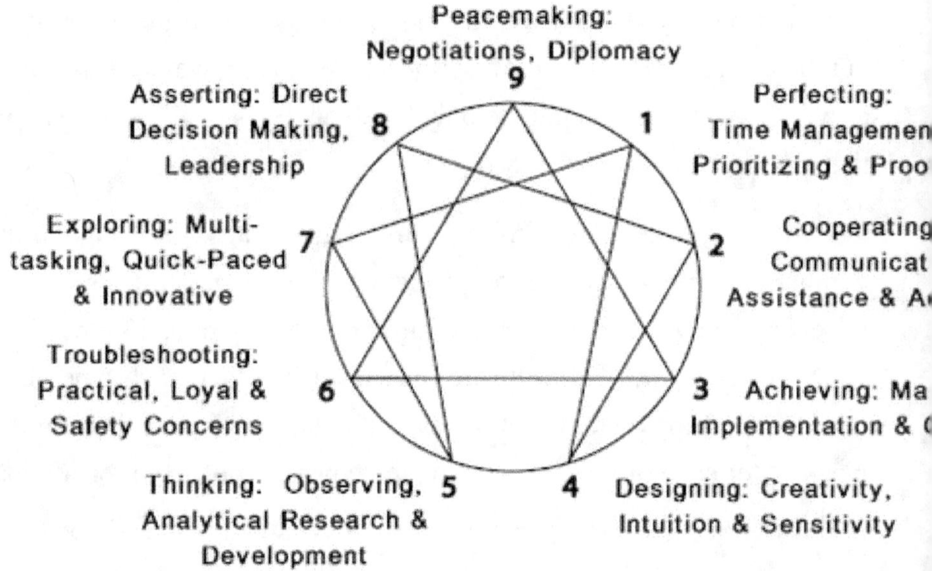

All nine types are guidelines that may present external attitudes and ways in which other people act. The enneagram tells you a lot about the general model, but it should not be taken literally. In fact, thanks to the interpretation and reflection of your data, it can give you an exact key to understanding the world around you. This means that you could find some types with some oddities, which may seem different from the description you will find here, and in any case you will find that most of the features are perfectly consistent with reality.

As you enter the world of the enneagram you will probably find various prospect figures with which you will feel similar. Your personality can fit into several types and this depends on a very important fact:

Your life is unique and has led you to go through very different periods. All people pass from one enneatype to another over the years.

But beware: what directs us towards the enneaty that we will keep is fear. In fact, fear is the source of almost all our actions. What we do or do NOT do almost always fear something. Do you want practical examples to understand?

- you have a job because you don't want to be without money and you want to pay for food and a home loan every day.
- you behave yourself because you don't want to have problems with the law.
- you are kind to your boss at work because you want to get a promotion and you don't want to be fired.

Obviously things as you know are a lot more complex, but the base is this. The brain has evolved to make us survive for as long as possible, so fear is one of its fundamental springs: avoiding damage is what we all want. Children face different unpleasant situations and during these small traumas they assume the characteristics of a certain enneatype. Then, after a while, people grow and stabilize for longer periods in a given enneatype. For example, if the thing that scares you the most is to be alone, you will tend to behave in order to have many friends. Everyone has a fear that is stronger than the others, and this directs the enneagram: it will have chosen an enneatype in a stable way. This will remain even as an adult, albeit in different ways. Our instinct then, our fear, will make us choose how to behave from then on.

Our enneatype is the social and intimate demonstration of what scares us the most.

These are the main fears of each enneatype:

Type 1 - be inadequate

Type 2 - be alone

Type 3 - fail

Type 4 - feelings

Type 5 - privacy violated

Type 6 - be deceived

Type 7 - getting bored

Type 8 - be part of the mass

Type 9 - lose your peace of mind

Many people live in states of constant anxiety and allow fear, worry and insecurity to dominate and define our lives. We allow these to deprive us of fun, sleep and our most precious dreams. If you want to achieve happiness and realize all your dreams, you must be ready to face all your fears.

The reason we prefer to keep it safe is the fear of looking ridiculous, of looking bad, of getting out of hurt, of confronting rejection or of failing. We learn to live with fear from childhood, due to traumatic experiences or negative messages that we see everywhere. Although fears are not our responsibility, only we can face them and eliminate them from our lives.

Let's talk about fear and how to deal with them. It may seem difficult, it can be frightening but once you have taken this road you will look back and wonder why you did not do it before. Now sit down, rest assured and read these super tips for your peaceful future.

1. Have you ever thought that if you become a friend of your fears these will no longer be so terrible? You already know what your fears are, so invite them into your lives. You have to find the courage to find yourself in situations that scare you, breathe deeply and take a leap. If you learn to go beyond your fears you will also understand the way to be comfortable with yourself and others in every situation.

2. Positive thinking is the most beautiful thing in the world. It may seem trivial, it may seem obvious, but it is above all true. The thoughts that relate to fear bring only more fear, so leave them behind. Instead of always expecting the worst, train your mind to see and hope for the best. Welcome to the best ideas for the future.

3. If you pay less attention to your fears, they will get smaller. Reflect on how you invest these three elements. The most important reason in the world in this sense is that we usually think and pay attention exclusively to something important and therefore we need to be conscious, prepared and focused on solutions that reduce the situations of fear.

4. Learn to value your successes. Fear is fueled by the failures and negative ideas that arise from the traumatic episodes of our lives.

For this reason, to face it, it is important to remember and know every victory you have had. We are not used to giving importance to our triumphs, when they should be our tool to impose new challenges and persist.

5. Don't be afraid to ask for help. Family and friends are one of the sources that generate more confidence. When you feel that you are about to be overcome by your fears, ask for help; certainly your loved ones will help you see the alternatives and possible risks.

6. A smile that defeats a fear, learns to defuse your fears and laugh. Our fears, real or imagined, feed on our insecurity. However, when we laugh at them and minimize them, we can see them from the right perspective. By making them the object of our laughter, we deprive them of their power; this will help us face the challenge and face them.

EXTRA ADVICE: Make a list of all the fears you managed to defeat. This will be a reminder of your ability to move forward; the next time you face a fear, consult the list and arm yourself with courage to increase it.

Do you think these pages are helping you to grow and improve your life? Very well, leave me a review on Amazon and recommend this book to other people who need to learn more about themselves and feel good.

IN-DEPTH ANALYSIS OF THE NINE TYPES

The time has come to understand more technically how the nine enneatipis are and how they can help you and the people around you.

The Enneagram consists of a circle that includes an equilateral triangle, which in turn intersects a six-sided figure. The points that touch the circle are numbered from one to nine in a clockwise direction and are connected by lines and arrows. These are the external signal that shows who wants to read the enneagram how one can migrate between the various represented personalities.

The Enneagram of psychological types is a "map" that describes nine types of personalities and the relationships between them, and that allows to identify the main tendencies of character, visions of the world and attitudes, as well as the most probable evolutionary hypotheses, allowing to increase the their own possibilities for self-understanding and inner transformation, with their own strengths and areas for improvement. Each personality represents the crystallization and adaptation of defenses in the process of early adaptation to the environment and is structured around an emotional nucleus, a cognitive nucleus and a nucleus that concerns the sphere of instincts that regulate human activity.

More than a mere classification, the enneagram is a dynamic model in which each enneatype encompasses the potential of all others, even if for each person there is a stronger identification with a certain type. It is important to emphasize that there is no better enneatype than another, or more fortunate in terms of personal resources: in the dynamics of the enneagram they are all rich in potential and, depending on their evolution or involution, they tend towards a certain type of positivity or of negativity characteristics. The nine personalities identified by the map are correlated according to a scheme that is depicted with a nine-pointed star and which expresses the relationship between the fundamental laws that move different personalities with the different characteristics.

This specific subdivision of a field into nine sectors with specific and recognizable characteristics, appears as a symbol-form that can be traced back to the image of the mandala, segmentation with more repetition of the various repetitions, a sort of oracular evocation of the modern concept of the fractal, anticipation of the ability to understand the reality that falls into the structure and becomes language.

Once introduced as a psychodiagnostic coding of character types, enenneagrammadella's personality was quickly introduced as an opportunity to read the human unfolding of behaviors, relational modalities and communicative forms, a model for reading "characters" or "archetypes of personality". The 9 types were compared with everything and more, subdividing new categories associated with as many pathogenetic conditions, psychosomatic correspondents, correlated virtues and vices with the respective ways and forms of evolutionary overcoming that the spirit offers.

Look around the street, the people around you are often weighed down by a deep sense of uncertainty. In fact, we all live in a world hit by social and international degradation.

This degradation is such that the individual who is affected ignores the fact that things are different, that is, he ignores the fact that a loss has occurred, a limitation, that it has become impossible to develop all its potential. The degradation of consciousness is such that awareness becomes blind to one's own blindness, and so limited as to believe itself free.

Think of your direct life experiences, think of the world in which every day you wander in search of something. What did you do yesterday? What are your main goals for your existence?

Maybe you don't really understand the scope of what I'm about to tell you but I want to ask you two questions and I want you to think very well of the answers you will tell me.

1. What aspirations did you have for the future when you were a child?
2. Five years ago, what did you think about your future?
3. And I also add a third question, I recommend it is important.
4. Are you the person you wanted to be ten years ago?

The character is structured according to a certain number of basic modalities, which translate into the relative predominance of one or the other aspect of the mental structure common to all. We can think of the "mental skeleton" of which we are all endowed as a crystal structure that can break in many ways, all predetermined; in the same way, among all the main structural characteristics, in the personality of each individual (as a result of the interaction between innate factors and environmental factors) only one of these structures will have prominence, while the others will remain on a more or less remote background. Another possible analogy is that of a geometric body that rests on one or the other of its faces; we all have the same personality with identical sides and vertices, but (and here is the analogy) oriented in space in a different way. There are, of course, nine possible dominant passions, each associated with a peculiar cognitive distortion, and there are also one, two or three characteristics derived, as I said, from the instinctual sphere. The nine types presented here are not just a mixture of personality styles; on the contrary, they are an organized set of character structures, as specific relationships, contrasts, polarities and relations of closeness are established between them.

The Enneagram is a theory that speaks of the interior of man in a very direct way. Although it may be useful to apply the knowledge of its laws to other people, it is much better to use it as a useful tool for a better understanding of oneself.

His knowledge acts as an incipit that introduces into the subject the glimmer of conflict, the awareness of the dissonance between his automatic mechanisms of action and reaction and his healthy part, which stands out and begins to move, to reflect, to observe the mechanisms themselves, to recognize them, to wish to free themselves from unhealthy automatisms, or rather those conditionings that remove the possibility of realization, and that begin to be recognized as undesirable.

The graphic representation of the Enneagram is that of a circle divided into nine points indicated from 1 to 9 in a clockwise direction, with the hour 1 of the quadrant coinciding with the 1 of the enneagram and the 12 of the quadrant which coincides with 9 .

The points are equidistant from each other and joined by lines that represent the internal relations of the system.

There are two lines of conjunction:

- Line 3-6-9 which forms an equilateral triangle.
- Line 1-4-2-8-5-7-1 whose digits constitute the periodic sequence obtained by dividing any of the other cardinal numbers by seven.

According to the theory of the Enneagram, a human being is born in a state of "essence". This state must be interpreted as a situation of pure potential in which every manifestation responds appropriately to the stimulus of the moment. In particular, since thought has not yet developed, it is instinctive / emotional responses that are completely free and guided only by the energy that is inherent in the creation itself.

In short, however, this state is completely lost: the opportunities / limitations of the environment produce a series of pressures that lead to "fixed" answers from which all subsequent functions will evolve. I believe, therefore, that even if the logical ego has not yet even formed in the child under twenty months of age, and therefore there is no center of reference, the instinctual part has already developed its own "reason".

This reason operates on an intuitive basis regulated by the instinct of adaptation and follows a fundamental criterion of expansion, which requires contact, or retraction, which involves separation or removal.

In this first phase the physiological apparatus of the deep brain, which supervises the emotional functions, is already almost completely developed and this means that everything that happens to the child also arouses two groups of fundamental primary instinctive / emotional responses (POLARITY) . These Polarities operate in a state of constant interactive flow and lead, over time, to developing the sense of reality in the child. The situation evolves dramatically with the birth of the ego or sense of identity.

From that moment on, being fully senses the sense of a separation between itself and the rest of the universe, its limitations, its sense of deficiency and tends to make up for all these shortcomings by immediately developing a defensive emotional system that reassures it and allow it to survive.

The two Polarities come, through the intervention of the instinct of adaptation, consequently reunited in a single emotional "fixed" response (THE PASSION), coherent with the claims of the environment in which the child lives (WOUNDED OR ORIGINAL DRAMA). In this way the natural instinctual homeostasis is completely lost, the instincts will be corrupted by the force of the passion and being, like an automaton, will continue to respond to the different situations that arise, always following the "program" that he had to adopt in the his original family situation.

The subsequent development of the logical function will not then modify the existing situation, since thought will also follow the path already taken by instinctual and emotional responses, and will jam in a way of thinking that will take into consideration only some aspects, refusing to see others unwanted (FIXATION).

The task of the man who wants to evolve is therefore to get out of this "mechanicalness", trying to reactivate those indispensable energies in order to overcome the ontic blackout I mentioned earlier.

it will be necessary to go through a first phase of recognition of the working methods of one's own mechanisms, a second phase of revisiting deep emotional experiences and replacing them with higher emotional forms called VIRTU 'and a final phase in which the primitive ego will have to replace a being evolved that has as its characteristic that to see the world in a not egoic way.

- Superbia (a display of one's own superiority over others).
- Avarice (lack of generosity, the one who is a stingy, but originally indicated the
- tendency to excessive and unjustified accumulation, hoarding).
- Lust (dedication to pleasure and sex).
- Envy (unhealthy desire for those who possess better qualities, goods or situations
- of its own).
- Throat (abandonment and exaggeration in the pleasures of the table).
- Wrath (easily letting go of anger).
- Sloth (laziness, idleness, the little desire to do, apathy, disinterest towards the others, towards themselves, and towards life).

In other words, what is called Personality, characterized by an Inferior Emotional Center (Passions), by an Inferior Intellectual Center (Fixations) and by corrupt Instincts, must replace a true and complete way of being Essential composed of Instincts naturally free, HOLY Virtues and Ideas.

Enneatips scheme

Enneatips scheme

- Types One avoid anger, do not get angry and tend to be perfect in everything
- Types Two avoid the sense of need, boast of being of great help to others and do not admit that they need others
- Types Three avoid failure, identify with the successes they get

- The Four types avoid ordinariness, they are always considered special
- The Five types avoid the void, always intent on increasing their knowledge
- Types Six avoid deviance, see life as ordered by laws, rules and norms
- Types Seven avoid pain, love fun and do not notice the pain of others
- Types Eight avoid weakness, boast of being strong and love to quarrel
- Types Nine avoid conflict, do not hold tensions between people and seek peace

ENNEATYPE ONE: CHARACTERISTICS

Type One is a person not inclined to accept anger and states of hatred in general, in fact he defends himself by doing the opposite of what he thinks or feels, and looking for the error outside of himself. In accordance with the principle that where there is passion there is also a strong sense of the forbidden, the person subjected to a specific passion does not seem to manifest the most evident characteristics of that passion, the word Ira is scarcely evocative of the characteristics of this type. The people who socially believe it possible to get angry for many things hardly lose their temper and it is indeed repugnant to them the spectacle of people who cannot control themselves or express themselves correctly. We are in the presence of people who have been the classic "good boy" and are from orderly, scrupulous, polite, very hard-working adults with a strict moral code. People who hardly raise their voices to impose themselves but who are very careful about how things are done and easily feel an inner sense of annoyance for those who, according to them, do not perform their duties with the due care. It can be said that anger arises in them precisely because others do not behave as they believe they should and how they do themselves. Anger is the only one of the traditional capital vices that is considered socially as having a double aspect. People of this type do not want to see in themselves the existence of the first aspect and identify fully only with the second. They have a vision of the world that proceeds according to criteria of right or wrong, black or white, dirty or clean and blindly believe that they are completely right when they make their judgments. This tendency to avoid any incorrect or ambiguous behavior leads them to cover their actions with an ethical veil of "good education". This leads them to use a phrasebook full of conditionals with which the angry person can present himself as a person animated only by good intentions. Phrases like: "You should do this", "It would be better if you behaved in this way", or "you should avoid these behaviors", abound in their vocabulary. The other to whom this exhortation is addressed realizes, however, from the tone of the voice and from the look, that behind the apparent benevolence there is a hardness and a rage that do not admit replies. The tendency to pursue a kind of "puritanism", both behavioral and social, pushes the angry to be, often, the worst enemies of themselves, requiring continuous attention (which goes as far as extreme fussiness), aimed at avoiding any possible carelessness or imperfection. The most typical way in which these people express anger is actually criticism, which works like a sort of safety valve in a pressure cooker. Criticism, which often assumes the character of a gruff grumble, is fueled by a marked sensitivity that leads people of this type to feel what is wrong and sometimes become very rigid. It is therefore useless to ask a Type One to do, for example, an explicit self-criticism of what others consider an error, because a One could not, even if he wanted to, admit to the world that he had acted wrongly or inappropriately. Given that the IRA is located in the upper part of the Enneagram, in the part that is at ease with the practical action, it will also be characteristic of these people an excellent manual skill and a marked autonomy. While giving a great value to their privacy and respecting that of others as a principle, the Types One control the behavior of others with excessive care and often exceed in giving advice even if the others have not the least solicited. A classic literary example of this form of manifestation is the Talking Cricket of Pinocchio's tale.

A classic example belonging to the artistic world is Harry Higgins, the male protagonist of the comedy Pigmalione by George Bernard Shaw, better known with the title of his film version My Fair Lady. The world of comics provides us with another excellent representative of this type in the character of Lucy Van Pelt, sister of that Linus who gives her name to the famous Schultz stripes. The world of cinema and literature offers many good examples that can facilitate the understanding of the internal dynamics of this type. In Mary Poppins we can observe the educational and corrective attitude combined with her expression full of good manners. The acting of Julie Andrews, also a type One, adds to the character's literary traits a vigor and a decision to set a good example for the children who have been entrusted to her, who perfectly render the style proper to Ira. Behind the famous words, "a little sugar is enough", it is clear that there is no real sweetness in imposing adherence to what is socially considered to be "good behavior". Instead, the attitude of Alister Stuart is extreme, the husband of the silent protagonist of Piano Lessons, a prisoner of his inability to reveal the real feelings he nourishes and at the same time is so controlled as to be filled with anger but inert to his wife's betrayal. The resentment and the tormenting jealousy that torture him can find their outlet only when he intercepts the message that his wife sends to his lover and learns that his wife wants to abandon him. His reaction is typically that of a One who does not want to admit to himself that he is in the grip of a furious rage. In fact, he cuts a finger to his wife, thus preventing her from being able to play and then in some way being able to communicate her feelings, but she does so with an action that seems to her conscience not vindictive, but fully justified because it is only corrective of a behavior mistaken. The desire to silence the inner critical voice "saving" at all costs the beings, no matter whether humans or animals, dear to a type One, is instead the deep spring that moves the behavior of Clarice Starling, the heroine of Il Silenzio of the Innocents by the writer Thomas Harris. In the plot of the film and the book from which it is taken, the motivation of the character played by Jodie Foster is not the simple fulfillment of one's professional duty, but a deeper need to find inner peace through an action (the rescue of a girl kidnapped by a serial killer who brings back to Clarice memories of her childish experience after her father's death), which can silence, at least momentarily, the inflexible claims of her super ego. In the final part of the book, after the girl was rescued, Clarice receives a letter from Hannibal Lecter, the crazy cannibal psychiatrist played by Anthony Hopkins whom she turned to for help in the investigation, which clearly shows what the real motivations were that pushed her. With great psychological insight Lecter writes to Clarice: "Well, Clarice, the lambs have stopped shouting? ... I wouldn't be surprised if the answer was yes and no. The scream of the lambs will stop for the moment. But, Clarice, the problem is that you judge yourself without any mercy; you will have to earn it again and again, blessed silence. Because it is the commitment that makes you move and understanding what your commitment is, the commitment for you will never end ". The obsessive and absurd attempt to improve, getting rid of those parts of the human being that are considered "dirty" or "animals", is instead the ultimate root of the actions of the protagonist of the story by Stevenson The Strange Case of Dr. Jekyll and Mister Hyde . The splitting of the personality of which the protagonist suffers is much more than a simple allegory of the human condition; it shows us how the reasoning for good / bad schemes of the type One, can lead in extreme cases towards the rejection of a part of itself and the consequent mental pathology.

ENNEATYPE TWO: CHARACTERISTICS

The type year Two is a person who tends not to recognize the personal, social, material or immaterial elements he needs. These people have at their disposal a particular weapon that is identified with repression, hysteria and loving image. Have you ever thought about what the word pride means?

It is a boundless, opinion of one's qualities, successes or condition. This definition certainly has the merit of directing us towards one of the most obvious features of the proud, the great sense of self, but it also has the defect of showing us this passion more as an idea, an opinion, that the person has of himself . In reality, the inner world of a proud person has little to do with the cognitive aspect and is totally dominated by instinctual and emotional perception. The type Two position in the Enneagram clearly tells us that it is the farthest from the Center of Thought and thus underlines the decisive dominance of the emotional part. The logical speeches and the subtleties of thought bore a proud man, who is instead all focused on the search for intense emotions and love. The most classic phrase of people of this type is: "I am important to you and you cannot do without my love". In accordance with this assumption types Two are perceived as very good people, ready to do everything to help the other (not, of course, the other in a universal sense, but in the smaller one of the people that interest him), nutritious , of good company and available. In this way the passion finds a decisive foothold to disguise itself, as we have also seen in type One, behind an attitude of benevolence. People of this type, while often having a strong social ambition, have a tendency to show an image of themselves that is very attractive and pretty because for them it is important to feel the interest of the other. For this they surround themselves with people who amplify their self-esteem by requesting help and advice. Proud people love cheerfulness, spontaneity, a flowery and delicate language, environments rich in emotional warmth and, at the same time, feel uncomfortable in sad, conventional and impersonal situations. The parameter they use to evaluate the world and people is that of sympathy or dislike and once they have made a judgment in this sense, it is extremely difficult to change their opinion. In this sense, it must be pointed out that it is not a question of simple stubbornness but of a deeper form of rebellion towards anyone who wants to limit their emotional freedom.

This psychic necessity of not feeling limited by social conditioning in the search for pleasurable emotions is the presupposition of another typical character trait of Two, the seductiveness.

This seductiveness is often unconscious and the person does not even realize that he is sending messages to that effect. Sometimes this creates situations on the verge of embarrassment and ridicule, because the other, to whom these implicit messages are addressed, feels authorized to make advances that seem, on the contrary, absolutely groundless in the eyes of the Two. In more general terms we can say that, in the Pride, this great freedom to feel and express emotions is obtained at the expense of their cognitive perception. Of all the types, the Two is the one that exercises less control over the impulses and makes its emotional "spontaneity" its own flag of life.

All that a Two perceives as irritating is frequently expressed in explicit terms of disapproval, but more often it is transmitted in a way that stimulates the feelings of guilt .. The other, obviously, besides perceiving that behind the "sweet" recommendations and concerns there is a specific need for Two and not one's own, feels the manipulative character of these maneuvers. Often this type is rightly reproached for being possessive and intrusive precisely because he believes that there is nothing wrong with expressing these feelings.

Another specific element of type Two is to love children in a visceral way. This character trait is the result of a projection of the Two which sees the child as a being still not conditioned, very needy of help and which cannot in any way constitute a threat to his freedom.

A problem that the sons of the two types frequently have, is precisely that of freeing oneself from a definitely affectionate parent but who continues to consider him as a "little one", his own forty-year-old offspring. The characteristics that we have seen to be present in type Two (emotional warmth, seductiveness, nourishment, extreme request for closeness, to be important for loved ones, etc.) are those that are more typically attributed to femininity in the Western world. It is therefore not surprising if this type is the one that presents, in percentage terms, the highest presence of women among its representatives

Napoleon Bonaparte because his figure exemplifies both great egocentrism and the certainty of being the savior of an entire nation. A tasty anecdote tells us that one day Napoleon was trying to take, with difficulty, a book placed on a high shelf. A grenadier seeing him in difficulty said to him: "Majesty, wait for the help that I am the greatest". Napoleon flashing it

with his eyes he replied: "Fool! Higher, not bigger ". It is well known that many of the promotions and donations made by him depended on sudden movements of his soul, positively struck by an act of courage or dedication, rather than by a well-motivated design. His strange habit of holding a hand in his waistcoat at chest height can be explained with the attitude of type Two to feel alive through the perception of what is the center of his being: the heartbeat.

On the same line we find the character of the royal Cleopatra, a woman in whom pride, the ability to communicate (she spoke five languages fluently), the great passion, seductiveness and unbridled ambition all contributed to making the capacity formidable of manipulation that is proper of the type Two. The very modalities of his death recall the continuous call of the Two to his own heart, since Cleopatra took her life not directly, but through the bite of a snake whose venom blocked the heartbeat. The literary character of Shakespeare's tragedy, Antonio and Cleopatra, is no less passionate or less manipulative than the real one. In the first act of the tragedy we can see both aspects in action when Cleopatra, fearing unconsciously having lost her influence on Antonio, sends him a messenger, since her pride would never allow her to show her need directly to the lover, who remind him of her desire. The words that Shakespeare puts into Cleopatra's mouth are so psychologically exact that it is worth reporting them here: Cleopatra (addressing the messenger): "Go and see where she is, who she is with, what she does. Don't say I sent you. If you find him melancholy, tell him I'm dancing; if he is cheerful, tell him that suddenly I felt sick. Quickly, and then come back ". The most famous cinematographic interpretation of this drama is certainly that with Liz Taylor and Richard Burton. In it, Taylor, who is also a type Two, adds a certain childish fragility to the characteristics of the character and a need for explicit encouragement that are also typical of the Pride.

The singer Madonna can be considered a modern transposition of the character of Cleopatra. She too was ambitious and always knew how to sell a seductiveness that does not care much about the judgment of others, an image of independence and a desire for emotional freedom that does not want to undergo any kind of conditioning and does not care much about social judgment. Among the actresses we cannot fail to mention our world-famous Sophia Loren and Anna Magnani for their roles rich in emotional impulsiveness and affective warmth.

The most concretely maternal and nourishing aspect of the Two is instead found, fully expressed in Mia Farrow, a great mom who does not pay for her natural children did not hesitate to generously adopt a colony of children of different nationalities.

ENNEATYPE 3: CHARACTERISTICS

Elementary Three has a strong fear of the feeling of failure and adopts a strategy of identification with the social values that the situation requires following an enhancement of the context and its deeper acceptance.

The behavior of these people does not consist, in fact, in a pleasure in telling lies to others but rather in telling them to themselves, trying to increase the sense of their existence and their value through a corresponding increase of their image.

The ability to do a lot and well, to get results at any cost, to correspond exactly to any role or gender image required by society, is what distinguishes this passion from that of the Pride that we have already examined.

The inability to have a clear sense of self and to understand feelings in depth, is instead the profound motivation that lies at the root of this passion. A famous Persian proverb states that a peacock without feathers is nothing but a big turkey and Vanitoso is someone who learned this lesson very early in his life, someone who feels inside himself that he has no value if he does not shine and is not a winning. In accordance with this belief, type Three works very hard and always tends to sell an image of itself that is taken care of down to the smallest detail, to take care of its appearance almost to become a cosmetic addict, to be a fitness fanatic and a connoisseur of right "timing".

Three sees the world as a place where it is not only necessary to compete but it is also indispensable to win; for this reason it manages to identify itself with the role it occupies and to change, like a chameleon, its own image.

Unlike the type One who is moved by an anxiety to do well, the type Three is moved by an imperious urge to do what can bring an advantage to himself (or to his loved ones), and is completely convinced that his way it is the only right one.

The desire to carry out one's projects is so strong that Three is characterized as a formidable organizer, motivator and seller of himself. Objections and perplexities are never readily accepted and the Three consider them only as a form of envy on the part of the losers.

In fact, these people often tend to have relationship difficulties with other people who feel little involved, if not even used as simple tools, in projects that Three is pursuing with tenacity. If this situation involves people who are deeply loved by them, the Three react with anger and a sense of painful astonishment, similar to what a Two can experience, which can also lead to more total emotional detachment to prevent sentimental disruptions from interfering with their ability to do. In more general terms, intimate relationships can be a real problem for people of this type.

Since the Three often fail to understand the deep emotion of their partner or their own, they tend to interpret the image of the perfect companion, knowing however that they are only playing a role. This difficulty of being in real contact with deep emotionality, which constitutes the most reliable source of the sense of being from an ontological point of view, can have devastating consequences on the life of a Type Three.

Which people from the international entertainment world can be defined as Type Three? The great chameleon-like ability makes Vanitoso the type most suited to playing roles. It is therefore not surprising if among the celebrities we find a long series of successful actors such as Laurence Olivier, Sharon Stone, Tom Cruise, Richard Gere, or singers who have found themselves at ease in acting film parts like Whitney Houston or Barbra Streisand.

The ability of the Three to be a highly skilled communicator and to use one's body as a tool to achieve successes beyond the artistic field is, instead, evident both in characters like Arnold Schwarzenegger and Sylvester Stallone who managed to become industry captains by selling a precise self-image, which in Ronald Reagan whose rise from second-rate actor to President of the United States is the most formidable parable of Vanity's motivational drive.

The great chameleonic ability of this type is, however, admirably expressed by actress Jane Fonda. Born in an environment of actors of strong political tendency radical (it is, in fact, daughter of Henry Fonda and sister of Peter Fonda, both actors very busy in the social field), she had fully adapted to the family values selling in her youth an image of pacifist fiercely opposed to the American capitalist system and the military intervention in Vietnam, to the point of giving its first son the name of Ho Chi Minh and of pronouncing a public anathema against the soldiers who were leaving for the war.

It is therefore not surprising that among the type Three artists we find people who see art as a means to appear, to emerge in society, offering what the dominant culture of their environment requires, rather than someone who is interested in 'absolute.

ENNEATYPE FOUR: CHARACTERISTICS

This type of people does not want to feel lost and hates the sense of despair. Precisely for this reason it avoids simple sadness and defends itself from the outside world trying to please others in an incessant search for love that never fails, however, to satisfy the person, since the refined superego of these people requires them not to never settle for anything less than perfect. The Type Four feels like a kind of angel fallen for its own demerit from Paradise and suffers a lot from this "bad" image of itself. Pain and guilt are consciously perceived and often lead to a tendency to lament and open or creeping depression.

The Invidioso always evaluates as the most important (no matter if people, things or situations), the one who does not have and there is not, rather than what belongs to him. Everything is ardently desired and perceived as indispensable, however, when it is finally obtained, it loses the attraction it seemed to have before. In this process ideality plays a leading role, since type Four is the one that most consistently compares the real situation with a model of unattainable perfection, detecting its shortcomings. This creates a characteristic and painful "push and pull" according to which, for example, only the best features of the partner are seen as long as it is far away, but not even the most minute imperfections escape when it is near. This attitude also leads to reliving emotionally all the situations of the past by covering them with a veil of sweet sadness and melancholy and, correlatively, always feeling that you have made wrong choices, thus diminishing the situations of the present life.

This existential attitude finds a natural outlet in artistic creativity, which is also a means to relieve the torment produced by the perception of one's own shortcomings. It is not, therefore, strange that this type is the one in which artists abound, in particular those linked to a vision that considers life as a form of universal pathos.

Empathy for the poor, the abused and the suffering is very much alive in this type, since the Type Four easily identifies with their condition.

Given the cultural model of our society, in which the male gender is the dominant one, many Type Four women have, on the basis of this sensitivity, participated in the forefront of women's emancipation movements.

At the same time, however, he would prefer to renounce everything but not his painful sensitivity by which he feels he is fully alive. For this reason the Four is the type that gives the greatest importance to the ability of others to decode the often elusive messages that hide behind the nuances of his behavior and believes that those who love him must necessarily understand his deep desires.

The high emotionality is also reflected on the humoral level, causing continuous and unmotivated ups and downs that reflect the sudden passages between moments of exaltation and an occult depression.

The artistic abilities of the Four make poets, novelists, singers, painters and actors abundant among such representatives.

Among the latter we immediately mention Marilyn Monroe who, despite being the symbol of female beauty in the collective imagination, was totally dissatisfied with her appearance. It is well known that Marilyn destroyed whole albums of photographs with scissors, always finding something that made her dissatisfied with the image she transmitted. In reality and in the typical manner of the Four, what made poor Marilyn despair was that no photo could express the deep pain of her heart; the desperate need for love that had remained unsatisfied throughout his life.

Very similar to that of Marilyn Monroe is also the human parable of James Dean, another famous actor who belonged to this type. Generally the actors of this type always manage to convey to the characters that interpret a romantic aura and a deep sensitivity, which are often absent in the scripts.

This is the case, for example, of Vivian Leigh in her famous interpretation of Rossella O'Hara, who is instead a quintessential Three type, by Robert De Niro in the film The Hunter (whose character according to the plot is instead a type Six) or in Raging Bull (where he plays the role of boxer Jack La Motta a type Eight), Judy Garland and Marlon Brando.

ENNEATYPE FIVE: CHARACTERISTICS

Kindness Five does not want to feel emptiness and is defended with the isolation of emotions from experience.

The emptiness in the lower part of the Enneagram indicates a decisive change of existential attitude between the positions marked at point Four and at Five. If, in fact, the Four is, as we have seen, marked by an ardent desire and by the hope of being able to change its state, Five has separated himself from his feelings and is deeply convinced that nothing can change for the better.

In envy, despair, which is still an emotional movement, is a seething hell of desire; here it is in a frozen hell that lies beyond the limits of despair itself. Avarice is, therefore, more than a passionate love for money and material goods (although, of course, there are also misers who are properly such in common language), a profound feeling of having little, combined with fear (the type In fact, Five is a satellite of the Six, which as we will see is dominated by Fear) of being able to lose what little we have. There is, yes, greed in this type, but it is so restrained by the fear of exposing oneself to some risk that a Avaro will hardly be able to convince himself that an action is necessary to get what one wants.

The metaphor I always resort to to explain this existential position is that of the shipwrecked person who, coming under the coast on his boat with few provisions, fears to jump into the water and walk along the stretch of sea that separates him from the shore, for fear of losing that little left to him. Here, continuing the metaphor, the foodstuffs are the vital energies that the miser feels he does not have enough to face the situations head on.

This feeling of weakness drives a miser to particularly fear sentimental complications and to defend his inner world by freezing every impulse, putting a defensive barrier between himself and the outside world. An almost inviolable sancta sanctorum in which to take refuge to calmly elaborate the events of life and a long time to respond to stimuli, are vital needs for a Five.

Separating himself from his emotions, however, and turning his life into a dry desert, Avaro separates himself from the primary source of perception of himself and feels, unconsciously, to live like a robot and to have betrayed the task that life has assigned to each of us.

From here comes a close to a pessimistic and sometimes cynical view of the world, a painful sense of guilt pervading and lucid that this type often warns like a curse weighing on itself.

A Five feels like a small, weak child surrounded by wolves, so he uses all his energy to escape or hide better. Therefore, he cannot bear to have the eyes of others on him, to expose himself, to be in the front row in the spotlight, to be asked something, and finds it particularly difficult to share his space with someone else. Generally an Avaro mainly uses his thought as a defensive factor against possible dangers.

Among all types, the Five is the one that is more at ease with the world of ideas, logic, intellectual controversy and less with the field of practical and material action. Even the image that others have of him is of little interest to a Five, who, typically, is detached from the desire for pleasure and from all that is only appearance.

The enormous desire to know makes it the prototype of the philosopher in his ivory tower, of the detached and impartial observer, of the astronomer, of the anatomist, of the scientist who, isolated in his laboratory, feels perfectly at ease. The loneliness that is so frightening to other types is, on the other hand, sought after and often desired by the Five who can, in this way, use his time to mentally tidy up the enormous quantity of information and knowledge he accumulates.

This enormous "head" continually at work, sucks in somehow all the vital energy and pushes the Five to try to save the maximum of itself.

The prevalence of the cognitive aspect explains why this type is the one that presents the greatest number of philosophers and scientists. Among the first we can mention men such as Pythagoras, Parmenides, most of the Cynics, of the Skeptics, Epicurus (who was not at all a hedonist), Seneca, Marcus Aurelius and St. Thomas Aquinas. The latter, in particular, was called by his confreres the silent ox, because he never took part in philosophical or theological disputes and remained alone apart for most of the time. When one day, however, his opinion was asked about a difficult passage in the philosophy of Aristotle, he interpreted it with such acuteness and precision that everyone was struck by his genius.

Among modern philosophers we can mention Hobbes, who argued among other things that life is nothing but a movement of the limbs and therefore that an automaton has its own life, Bergson, Leibnitz, Heidegger, Popper and above all Descartes. Some choices of his life that may seem surprising, are perfectly explained by knowing the Enneagram. Thus it is not difficult to understand why the agricultural company that his father had left him as a legacy was undone (too much effort was needed to carry it forward), preferring, in exchange, a modest fixed annual income. In Paris he found the life of society boring and too energy-consuming, preferring to isolate himself in a monastic district, to devote himself to the study of geometry.

The lucid and irreversible despair that often strikes the Five is, however, very evident in the works of two of the greatest writers belonging to this type: Franz Kafka and Emily Dickinson. Both deeply convinced of the impossibility of changing their state for the better and of being able to participate fully in the gathering of other humans, they expressed this pain with words of lucid anxiety, so profound that it could not even allow crying or hope.

ENNEATYPE SIX: CHARACTERISTICS

Type nine fears to deviate from the group's norms and defends itself by projecting unacceptable emotions onto others.

The Fear was, as I have already pointed out in the introductory part, one of the two passions not included in the traditional list of Sins or Capital Vices. This was probably due to two different reasons. On the one hand, in a medieval Christian perspective, fear, or fear of God, was not considered a negative element, since it, through the memory of judgment and eternal punishment, led man to subject himself to the law and to the social order. On the other hand it must be said that the very dynamics of this passion were not well understood.

The variety of behaviors induced by the passion of Fear, in fact, is such that, at first sight, there seems to be little in common among many people belonging to this type. If, in fact, it is rather easy to understand that people who are commonly referred to as phobics are certainly dominated by Fear, those, in other words, who have a lifestyle dominated by insecurity or phobias in part explicit, is not just as easy to see at a motivational level the fear in those people called counterphobic, who act with a strong strategic aggression.

This reaction is obviously not due to a form of courage, but to an instinctive defense that is put into action by Fear.

In the game of chess to express this concept well, we use the following saying that effectively focuses on the inner world of a Pauroso, "the threat is much stronger than its execution". With this expression we mean to point out that the idea of a risk that hangs over us, can be much more unbearable for our psyche, than the fact of actually facing the danger itself. Most of the Six, despite being mainly phobic or counterphobic, show in their behavior traits of both reactions.

This typical alternation extends to almost every possible behavior and is often described by the term ambivalence.

However, there is a further possibility of expressing the fear that can also be inferred from the behavior adopted by many animals within their group. In fact, in many species there is a special form of recognition of the superiority of the other, which takes place through a series of acts with which the authority of the dominant specimen is recognized and, at the same time, its place in the social scale is defined. of the group. In this way, each member of the group knows, on the basis of this precise order, exactly what his role is.

The fearful, in general, are very cerebral people, in the sense that they think too much about the possible repercussions of each single act, and they fight their insecurity requiring support and support and through a tendency to prefigure every possible scenario. For this type it is decisive to know what is the behavior required by the authority and, with their typical ambivalence, to know how to behave in front of the requests that come from it.

We will thus have three distinct behaviors that have, however, in common the fact of having all originated from the need to suppress fear. Unlike a Five, a Six has not separated from his feelings and desires, but does not know if he can trust them (in the sense that he is never sure of the reactions that others will have), or if he can afford to express them freely.

A central theme for this type is that of the accusation and, just to avoid possible faults, the Six feel the need to know every single detail of a given situation.

The Six does not easily grant its trust and is very careful in grasping the signs of ambiguity or disloyalty.

He often puts others (in particular his loved ones) to the test because his intimate ambivalence leads him to doubt even himself and his loyalty. The Fearful feels any small crack like a trap that could lead to complete collapse and therefore tends to be a lucid pessimist, who prefers to imagine the worst to be ready for any eventuality.

As for illustrious examples of this type of people we mention Raskolnikov's character, the fruit of Dostoevsky's pen who was also a Six, shows in the succession of the novel's events both the implacable strength that the prosecution has in the mind of a fearful , is the wobbly journey that can lead people of this type towards liberation. The same path as Raskolnikov, but at a much higher level, is the path taken by the fisherman Simone di Giovanni, who from the guilt of having betrayed, three times his messiah, out of fear, in a night full of anguish and confusion, assurs, through the experimentation of grace, at the level of the first among the faithful of the new religion of Christ.

The episode, handed down by the Christian tradition, of the Quo Vadis, shows us, however, how Fear is, perhaps, the most tenacious and pervading human sentiment and, correlatively, like the example and reassurance of an authoritative figure is always for a You are a blessing that can suppress any Fear and lead to the highest degrees of transcendence.

ENNEATYPE SEVEN: CHARACTERISTICS

The seven-year-old type escapes from suffering by intellectualizing and sublimating emotions into a vortex that many know as sins of greed. It is something far more pervasive and subtle than the common use of the word greedy may suggest. Given the position of this type on the Enneagram, one can immediately understand how the cognitive aspect is the prevailing one and that, therefore, the Throat is more a taste for the intellectual promises of a situation, than a simple taste for food or cooking refined (even if, as for the other passions, there are greedy ones who are such in the common sense of the word). This passion is, therefore, definitely a desire to fill up with good things, but these "things" pertain more to the field of ideal expectations than to that of material.

The words hedonistic and epicurean that are often used in connection with this type, can only convey the tendency of the Seven to derive delight from their own actions and life, regardless of other interests or moral ends, but does not show that behind this apparent playfulness, there is a very strong component of fear that is somehow exorcised.

The Seven define themselves, and indeed they are, as lovers of life, cheerful, carefree, optimistic and convinced that there is always a solution to every problem, but they are the first to know that this layer of golden paint just covers the deeper feelings of loss and existential insecurity that are always lurking.

Like a child who put on a carousel, he fears that at the end of the race he may find himself completely alone without knowing what to do, a Seven is all oriented to find other ways to continue the duration of that game or to pass to other infinite, possible, games .

The greatest danger for a Seven is that of boredom, since the excitement easily leaves the place to a form of disappointment similar to that which the Four experiences. For this reason we can understand why the Seven is more interested in the game of conquest than in the results of the same.

The field of attention of a Seven is very vast but, typically, superficial and therefore the Greedy can be interested in anything, but only with extreme difficulty it will become really an expert, contrary to the Five to which it is connected by the inner arrow.

On the other hand he develops a very strong intuition that leads him to always find the best way to deal with interpersonal relationships and to be, sometimes, a fascinating liar. This habit of always being pleasant can easily be confused with the analogous attitude adopted by the Three towards the people he wants to like, but in the Seven there is a greater spontaneity and, above all, a more immediate emotionality. The accusation of being a little too light (or worse) so often moved to this type, often finds a confirmation more in the vision of itself that has a Seven, than in the objective reality of the facts. Curiosity is the additional fuel that drives the emotional machine of the Seven, making it believe that behind every novelty there can be the opportunity for a pleasant experience.

The most carnal tendency of the Seven is, instead, well expressed in the works of the great Federico Fellini and still more clearly in those of Tinto Brass (both types Seven in real life). In a memorable scene from the film Amarcord, the protagonist's grandfather manages to transmit to us in a quintessential way the idea that a Seven has death.

The women with huge breasts of Fellini's imagination are, like the women represented by the painters Rubens and Botero, an evident transposition of the irresistible attraction of the Seven towards an opulence that privileges quantity over quality.

More generally, it can be found in the works of the numerous directors (in addition to those already mentioned we can mention Robert Altman, Rob Reiner, Bob Fosse, Kenneth Branagh, Roberto Benigni and Steven Spielberg), the typical tendency to favor oneself in the memory of a experience the positive aspects, compared to the negative ones. Thus in Reiner's film Stand by Me the story points out the excitement and thrill of the young teenage protagonists, in search of their final maturity, rather than the feelings relating to the two deaths that are the main theme of the film.

La Vita è Bella by Roberto Benigni clearly illustrates the great ability of Seven to transform any situation, even the most tragic, into play. In the hell of the concentration camp, the protagonist manages to preserve his own son from the horrors and destruction of war, turning distressing situations and the fear of the present into an object of amusement.

A similar sensation can be felt in the most brilliant pages of Wolfgang Amadeus Mozart. The more difficult and economically heavy the real situations of his life were, the more his music became cheerful and carefree. Correlatively, in moments of greater tranquility, his music took on more serious and deep tones. In Mozart, the tendency of this kind to remain, fundamentally, a teenager on a psychological level.

Hugh Hefner, a typical Seven, claimed to have founded the famous Playboy magazine to escape from a real world of duty in a free zone of pleasure where all the fantasies were possible. The light and libertine Seven, however, can, by exemplifying the existential message of Tantra, transform his sexual energy into the spiritual one and thus become a person of transcendent and high morality.

Many of the great Sufi masters of history (Omar Khayyam, Jalaluddin Rumi etc.), have traveled this road reaching the highest peaks of human spirituality.

ENNEATYPE EIGHT: CHARACTERISTICS

Type eight refuses weakness and avoids defending itself with denial. This passion was considered by Christian writers, according to the classic tripartite division of the soul carried out by Greek philosophers, as a vice of the concupiscent part, capable of subjecting the spiritual side of man to the values of the crudely material sphere. In this way it was concretely linked to carnal relations and assumed the classic name of Lussuria, from the Latin word luxus (luxury), indicating, like the nearby

Gola, an inclination to find satisfaction in the things of the world, thus losing the ultimate meaning of 'existence.

Beyond the religious view, however, the deepest sense of this passion is not so much in the continuous search for sexual satisfaction (even if, as for the other passions there are some Lusts that are such in the common sense of the word), but it consists rather, in a pervading subjection of the emotional and cognitive parts to the force of every kind of desire.

In type Eight, every instinct is strengthened with a charge that leads him to not want to hear and consider any kind of inhibition.

This process in some individuals is emphasized beyond normal consideration and beyond all limits. The eight types are people who do not follow the rules and who live in an existential position in which every experience must be, so to speak, extreme.

A first corollary descending from this way of seeing is that which considers the world as an arena in which only the strong has the possibility and the right to satisfy itself. This person is the type that gives the most value to strength and power and, correlatively, takes little sweet sentimental expressions, which could weaken his reactivity. Although the fundamental inclination to pleasure makes this type surely a narcissist, Eight is not too interested in selling a pleasing image of itself, preferring instead to reveal its firm determination from every expression. The tendency towards fraudulence and manipulation that we have seen in the Seven, are also present in the Eight, which fails, however unlike the first, to mask the depth of its reactions very well.

Very at ease with his body and with great energy, the Eight does not hesitate to use his anger both as a control tool and as a means to instinctively judge the reactive capacity of others. Linked to his "extremist" vision of the world, Eight is very direct in both verbal and physical expressions, and is someone who hardly goes unnoticed.

Often the behavioral hardness and the declared aggressiveness are sought consciously by a Eight, as a further form of demonstration of one's invulnerability to pain, regardless of the damage or harm they can cause to others. In general, this type prefers to deal with a strong adversary, with whom he can possibly have a fight without exclusion of blows, rather than confronting enemies acting behind him, avoiding direct confrontation.

The closeness to the Nine expressed by the position of the Eight in the Enneagram, reminds us that even in this type there is a profound psycho-spiritual inertia in work, which typically leads an Eight to be little interested in his own inner world. On the other hand, however, the Eight has a vision that immediately captures the hypocrisy of a situation, the incongruity that cloaked in moralism what too often is nothing other than a form of prevarication of the strong over the weak.

From this point of view, Eight is the most revolutionary of all kinds and like the Four, at the antipodes in the Enneagram, easily takes the parts of the weaker against authority. The difference between the two types is that the Four acts in this way because it does not want a lower and a superior to exist, while the Eight, identifying himself with the weak, rebels against the limiting and repressive authority, perceived as illegitimate. Paradoxically, however, an Eight can easily behave like a dictator if he becomes the holder of power.

The characteristics of combativeness and the desire to demonstrate that it is the strongest, make the Eight the ideal prototype of the gladiator, of the fighter, of the fighter. It is not surprising, therefore, that some of the greatest boxers of all time are of this type and that some of them have been those who have most revolutionized the noble art. Among the many we mention Cassius Clay (Muhammed Alì after his conversion to Islam), Carlos Monzon, Jack La Motta, whose character was played by Robert de Niro in the film Toro Scatenato Roberto Duran and the recent, controversial former world champion heavyweights, Mike Tyson.

In team sports, Eight ability to be a leader and a formidable leader has been magnified above all by Diego Armando Maradona. Probably considered the greatest player of all times Maradona, born and raised in a very poor suburb of Buenos Aires, exemplifies better than anyone the great qualities of Eight wrestler and, at the same time, the difficulty of this type in giving himself a moral discipline and in containing the desire within acceptable limits. Abuse in drug use, excessive sexual desire (we recall the many stories that have filled the pages of newspapers and have seen it involved), and the tendency to satisfy oneself through excessive recourse to food and various stimulants have undermined prematurely the physique of this extraordinary champion, capable like many other Eights of arousing the most contrasting feelings of boundless admiration and fierce blame.

The tendency to subvert the established rules of this type is well shown in the world of art from the life and work of the painter Michelangelo Merisi, called Caravaggio. This innovative genius, who died only thirty-seven years after a dissolute and turbulent life that led him to various countries to escape arrest for murder, remains in the history of painting for the dramatic veracity of his representations and the importance and use of human body in the composition. As a good Eight (which we remember belongs to the triad of the Center of Action dominated by the belly), Caravaggio took as models for his works and depicted in the paintings, with an absolutely surprising realism and violence, real commoners with all their deformities and ugliness . Disrupting the mannerist taste of the time, Caravaggio introduced in his work the principle of the centrality of the real body and, through the use of a powerful play of lights and shadows, he managed to convey in his works a sense of drama and strength that reflect the profound conception of the life of an Eight.

In general, artists belonging to the Eight always leave a trace of the centrality of the body in their work. This is easily seen in the powerful and at the same time splendid forms in the design of other numbers Eight illustrious figures such as Benvenuto Cellini and Picasso.

ENNEATYPE 9: CHARACTERISTICS

The Enneatype Nine avoids conflicts through narcotization and glamor of conscience. The existence in Italian of the word Accidia, from the Greek Achedia not caring, allows us to express the essence of this passion much better than we can do with the use of the equally used Idleness or Laziness. In the type Nine there is certainly a form of laziness, but this more than a non-action often takes the form of a psycho-existential inertia, a bustle in a thousand things of no importance, always doing what is asked by others, a not wanting to make distinctions between what is essential and what is of little importance. The strategy implemented at an unconscious level to accomplish these goals can alternatively include both sleep and an exasperated structuring of one's time, by engaging in so many things of little or no importance. The slothful, therefore, is typically accommodating and always ready to take on the heaviest workload (even if this costs him, in any case, not a little in terms of fatigue), even if he does not have to stop and think about the things he does .

Ultimately we are faced with a psychic position that leaves no room for the profound needs of the person, who accepts to subordinate himself to the needs of the partner, the family or, more generally, the group to which he belongs. From this point of view the Nine can easily be confused with the Two, which implements a similar attitude, also because both types believe they can "do without".

In the Nine, however, the aspect of giving is lacking in order to have and, instead, a form of psychological passivity is expressed which expresses the unconscious denial of one's anger. The most typical forms with which the Nine express their repressed anger are, in reality, stubbornness and forgetfulness of people and problematic situations.

Another typical aspect is that of justifying oneself, if the relationship or the situation does not go well, saying: it is not my fault, I did nothing.

In all the Enneagram literature, the Nine is considered the type that best expresses the real human condition on the spiritual level; the passion in which the subtle difference that exists between a consciousness that forgets the things of the world goes towards the transcendent, and an ego that forgets itself loses itself in the world of material, finds its most evident expression.

The practical sense and the easy accommodation to the things of the world of the Nine type, appear evident in the figure of Sancho Panza, the immortal squire of the Engineer Don Quixote of La Mancha (a type Six with a very strong Seven wing), which unlike his more than an idealistic master, he explains with these words to his wife, who asks him about his behavior, what is for him the real meaning of going after Don

Quixote: It is true that most adventures do not succeed as one would like, because of a hundred ninety-nine they end up backwards; nevertheless it is a beautiful thing to cross mountains, penetrate the forests, trample the cliffs, visit the castles and above all, stay in inns without paying a single penny. Sancho appointed as a joke governor of the so-called Barrataria island shows good judgment and discernment in judgments, but faced with an imaginary enemy invasion, he does not hesitate, when the apparent danger has passed, to strip himself of all his charges and resume with simplicity his original role.The same minimalist and almost renouncing attitude of Sancho Panza can be found in numerous other Nine literary, among which Bartleby the scribe deserves a mention, protagonist of the homonymous tale by Hermann Melville and Giorgio Babbitt the main character of the novel by Sinclair Lewis, quintessential prototype of the narrow-minded and traditional but not bad provincial American, who tries to escape the deep boredom that oppresses his existence by losing himself in a thousand jobs and considerations of little or no account. Babbitt expresses in particular another characteristic of the Nine that can easily be confused by greed: that of being surrounded by many objects and often collecting them. What moves the Nine in this behavior is, in reality, the need to not have to create a problem if something, for example, breaks down. The passivity, the easy giving in to the claims of loved ones and the stubbornness of the Nine in maintaining their position, appear evident in the Manzonian character of Lucia Mondella, whose innocence succeeds in striking in the deepest part of the soul the dusky but not insensitive Unnamed . The scene in which Lucia, despite disagreeing, gets her mother and Renzo to marry her by saying in front of a surprised Don Abbondio, the marriage formula, is true only if there is a Nine type to undergo that decision.

More determined and apparently vain, on the other hand, appear characters like Shakespeare Falstaff or Winston Churchill. The latter, who with his large body volume, even physically represents the stereotypical image of Nove, believed, in reality, to be very vain (in the sense, of course, common of the term), for his relative care of the image of if. The deep core of his personality, as he explained it himself in his autobiography, was, instead, typically Nine. Among the various interesting notes of Churchill's Nine being there is also the invention of the English tank called Tank. This stocky and massive vehicle, which had no stylistic claim, was somehow a form of unconscious projection of its author. The sense of equality of the Nine is fully expressed in the Constitution of the United States, whose founding fathers largely belonged to this type (and we can mention among others Benjamin Franklin and George Washington). The fundamental concept of the United States Declaration of Independence which, it is worth remembering, was promulgated when in the rest of the Western world almost absolute sovereigns reigned everywhere, it clearly states that we are all created equal and that, therefore, does not exist someone who has more rights than another.

The natural reluctance of the Nine to show off and his passivity sometimes pushed up to the catatonia, explain why the quiet and inconspicuous sixteen year old Albert Einstein, was considered little more than a retarded by his masters of the Aarau gymnasium who advised him to enroll in a vocational school and leave high school. Fortunately, Einstein had the typical stubbornness, in this positive case, of Nine and held firm to write books that changed the history of physics forever. In the award-winning film Dances with Wolves Kevin Costner shows us another aspect of the Nine type. Costner hero in spite of himself, asks as a prize a destination in close contact with the Sioux

Indians, whom nobody wanted to accept, because he wants to know the frontier before it disappears.

So far you have had access to this information through important information about this ancient art of the Enneagram. If you think their knowledge can really help you improve your life, then leave a review on Amazon and let everyone know.

ENNEAGRAM TEST: FIND OUT YOUR TYPE

Being aware of your own enneatype is mainly used to understand your strengths and all the limitations that you have to manage every day. Knowing your enneatype is essential to emphasize your merits in the second. Below is a test that allows you to quickly check your enneatype. For each question there are 9 answers, each of which belongs to a specific enneatype (the figures you find in brackets).

All you have to do is choose the answer that best reflects your personality and include the relevant number in the empty field at the end of the question.

To conclude you will have to detect the number that appears a number of times greater: your enneatype will correspond to that figure.

1. TO FEEL GOOD WITH ME I HAVE:

Helping others (2)

Be efficient, practical and be successful in my goals (3)

Know and learn as much as possible (5)

Being "diligent" and doing my duty (6)

Do everything to the best of my ability (1)

Have fun, be cheerful, enjoy life as much as possible (7)

Being strong and defending the right causes (8)

Be "different", stand out from the crowd (4)

Rest and let life flow calmly (9)

2. WHAT I THINK OF ME:

I move first if there is someone to help (2)

I am an efficient person, who tries to do everything well (3)

I distinguish myself from others in everything I do (4)

I am calm calm and satisfied with my life (9)

I am perceptive and understand things well (5)

I am strong and authoritatively manage my relationships (8)

I am ordered and always do my duty (6)

I like it and try to have fun and enjoy life (7)

I think I am right most of the time (1)

3. I FEEL REALIZED WHEN I CAN BE:

Original, Friendly, Wise (4)

Sensible, Accurate, Receptive (1)

Loyal, Disciplined, Trusted (6)

Optimistic, Sociable, Pleasant (7)

Impartial, Solid, Superior (8)

Placid, Harmonic, Balanced (9)

Direct, Accurate, Precise (5)

Affectionate, Generous, Helpful (2)

Winner, Expert, Practical (3)

4. SOMETIMES THE OTHER PEOPLE DO NOT UNDERSTAND YOUR THOUGHTS. WHAT DO YOU THINK WHEN THIS HAPPENS?

I am a reliable person and I stand by the rules even if others do not fit (6)

I'm happy, but I'm looking for new things because I want to be more (7)

I fight every day to get my space; I have to take it, otherwise the others take advantage of it (8)

I let my world go the way it goes, even if others would like me to work to change it (9)

I am often right and things would be better if you follow what I say (1)

I love others, even if I don't receive as much good as I give (2)

I rise above the others and this makes them jealous (3)

I stand out from the others and feel that I cannot really adapt to the world around me (4)

I can understand things better than others and nobody knows how many I know (5)

5. WHAT MUCH MORE AVOIDED:

Show my weaknesses (8)

Clash with someone (9)

Giving in to anger (1)

Need someone's help (2)

Show my mistakes (3)

A life without emotions (4)

The feeling of inner emptiness (7)

Having the wrong behavior (5)

The fatigue of living (6)

6. WHAT DO I THINK IF I ENTRUST AN IMPORTANT DUTY?

I don't give myself peace until I've realized how much I owe (1)

I am flattered that they have searched for me and will do more than requested (3)

They couldn't choose a better one than me and I advertise it (7)

It depends on how I feel (4)

Why did they look for me? However I do (5)

I'm afraid they chose me because there were no others; I will help you do it (6)

I do it if I like it, otherwise I try to download it to someone (8)

I can do it well, if it depends only on me (2)

As soon as I feel I do it (9)

7. HOW I WORK DURING A LITIGIOUS AND A DISCUSSION:

I hardly admit I was wrong (3)

I prevent the other from disturbing my inner balance (9)

I try to take time to meditate on a reaction (6)

I fight, but only to defend myself from the strength of those in front of me (4)

I try to avoid confrontation, most of the time it's not worth fighting (7)

I prevent the other from taking advantage of me (5)

I let the other vent (2)

I strongly defend my reasons (8)

I don't make my anger clear to the other (1)

8. I WANT TO COMMIT MY FORCES FOR:

Knowing what surrounds me (5)

Collaborate with those I have next to me (6)

Enjoy the joys of life (7)

Fighting for justice (8)

Live peacefully (9)

Seeking perfection (1)

Help those around me (2)

Reach my goals (3)

Know myself (4)

9. WHEN I AM WITH FRIENDS:

I always look for new ideas to share with many different (7)

I'm with those who let me talk (8)

I am expansive and let myself be pampered (2)

I like clear and precise relationships (1)

I like it, but if I am many I don't know who to choose (6)

I immediately find something of what I did to show them (3)

I find myself alone with those who have feelings with me (4)

I listen to them very carefully, but without putting too much of my (5)

I feel safe and I get over my normal attitude too (9)

Now look carefully at the answers you have given and read them aloud. What is the number that appears most frequently in your answers?

That is the number of your enneatype.

If there is not a figure that occurs more, it is necessary to recompile the test by choosing the answers more carefully.

GOOD ADVICES FOR EVERYONE

The enneagram helps to find the forces you need to cultivate and indicates the direction to follow by developing the positive qualities of our personality type. In this way the enneagram is very useful because it helps us to understand our strengths and our weaknesses; it helps us to know what price we will have to pay in the long term if we continue to enlarge our inner world and avoid growth and it helps us to know with certainty that there is a positive way of living, thus arriving in a dimension of inner serenity and atmosphere of improved sociality. If we want our change to go in the direction of growth, we must learn to desire what is truly right for us and have the courage to rebel against our fears.

<u>Advice for personality 1</u>

1. Learn to find a dimension of true relaxation. Give yourself time for yourself, without thinking that you have to do everything and that if you don't do something it will be chaos. The salvation of the world does not depend only on you.
2. You are good teachers and have much to teach, but do not expect others to change immediately. What is obvious to you may not be so for others. If they do not change immediately it does not mean that they cannot change later. Your words and your example can do a lot.
3. Do not preach. You yourself are not free from defects, stop examining others and acknowledge your defects.

4. Get in touch with your feelings and your unconscious impulses. It may be helpful to keep a journal or to start therapies and group work, both to develop your emotions and to see that others do not condemn you if you have human needs and limitations.

5. Your weak point is the anger that comes from feeling more virtuous than others. You easily get angry for what seems to you the perverse refusal of others to do the "right thing" as you define it. Beware of assuming the role of judge and moralizer. Your anger could bring you an ulcer or hypertension.

6. Learn to accept that others are what they are and decide for themselves. Don't always tell others what is "right" for them to do. Know how to discern wisely when to say and how to say, based on what the other can accept.

7. Listen to others: they too are often right. By listening you will learn more and become better teachers.

8. Stop being perfectionists: there is no precise way to wash dishes, to iron a shirt or to do other things. Avoid being picky.

9. Don't be obsessive in your thoughts and forced into your actions. Do not have an excessive sense of order, try to understand what is troubling you and do not waste your energy on small annoyances.

10. You don't need to be perfect to feel good, the best thing is to find your humanity.

Advice for personality 2

1. Ask yourself what others need and then help them pursue it.
2. Be generous without worrying about the exchange.

3. Try to gain awareness of your ulterior motives: your tendency to control others.

4. Resist the temptation to draw attention to your good works.

5. Do not try to earn the love of others by giving undeserved gifts or praises.

6. Looking for new friends is not always the solution to feeling good.

7. When you do something for others do it without them noticing and you will also benefit you and your soul.

8. Do not be possessive with friends, share them with others. There is enough love for everyone.

9. Make sure the reasons that lead you to help others are uninterested.

10. Love others for what they are and not for what they represent for you or for the opportunities they can guarantee you with their social status.

Advice for personality 3

1. Develop a deeper sense for cooperation in your relationships. Do not try to subdue others, to exclude them, to be snobs. Take into consideration their needs and feelings.

2. Don't overdo your importance. Be sincere and authentic people.

3. Be trustworthy. Keep secrets and confidences and resist the desire to use them to your advantage. Falsehood is an emotion that is not good for you.

4. Always be aware of your tendency to feel entitled to get what you want at the expense of others. Do not use others, do not take advantage of situations.

5. We must not change to please others.

6. Support others and encourage them. Instead of seeking attention and admiration, give it to others when they deserve it.

7. Use your great energies, sense of humor, organization, animation, panache for the benefit of the groups you belong to and individuals, making sure that they too are developing their best qualities.

8. Do not overdo it in wanting to be acclaimed.

9. Competition with others causes you discomfort.

10. Develop your spiritual potential. Do not get distracted from confronting anyone and don't worry about others' success.

Advice for personality 4

1. Generally you are too busy with your feelings.

2. Avoid postponing things, you don't need to have the right mood to do something. It is far better to maintain contact with the real world than to seek enlightenment.

3. Self-esteem and self-confidence will develop only by experiencing positive experiences, regardless of whether you believe you are ready to face them or not.

4. Use healthy self-discipline, learn to strive and work harder to stay healthy and achieve your goals.

5. Avoid giving yourself to sexual excess, alcohol, sleep or fantasies.

6. Talk openly with someone you trust. You will discover that you are not as different and as foreign as you feel you are.

7. Community service will make you less shy and awkward and make you feel better.

8. Do not let yourself be overwhelmed by self-pity or by complaints to parents, by thoughts of your unhappy childhood, by bad relationships or by the fact that nobody understands you. Don't continually undermine your self-esteem.

9. Don't do anything personal, don't be touchy or hypersensitive. After all, a critical remark is not the whole truth about you. Speak frankly and spontaneously and don't let others take advantage of you.

Advice for personality 5

1. Do not put preconceptions to reality and observe it. Analyze less and try to see things for what they really are.
2. Meditation, jogging, yoga, dance are useful for you.
3. You lack the sense of perspective, you see many possibilities and you don't know how to choose or judge.
4. Do not rush the conclusions. Do not be prejudicially anchored to previous ideas, give another opportunity to people.
5. Emotionally open yourself to friends, be truly open to people, it will greatly help you.
6. Try to be cooperative and less lonely. Educate other people, it will be instructive for you.
7. Don't make others feel uncomfortable, don't forget the social conventions that help others feel at ease with you.
8. Avoid looking down on those you think are less intelligent than you.
9. If others begin to avoid you or react antagonistically with you, consider the possibility that it started with you.

10. You have an enormous capacity for understanding. Think of ways you can develop compassion for others.

Advice for personality 6

1. Anxiety is not a merit nor an excuse to do what you want. Learn to use your anxiety and above all to manage it in the best way to always be able to understand and face the challenges of every young person.

2. Try not to be on the defensive and not to be irritable. Do not blame others for things that you yourself have done or determined. Resist the tendency to think negatively and whine because no one will tell you that you are the most beautiful or the best if you place yourself in the same position as a child who wants his toy.

3. Learn to identify what leads you to overreact. Things are not as black as you paint them and you have attracted them with your attitude.

4. Strive to trust more and enter into intimacy, run the risk of being rejected, it's worth it. Tell people what your feelings are about them.

5. The opinion that others have made of you is better than you think. You have unjustified fears.

6. Accept responsibilities with more maturity. People respect those who take responsibility, especially if they have made a mistake.

7. It is better to focus on the goal of affirming yourself, developing genuine confidence in your abilities. Develop good reasons to trust your abilities.

8. Do not worship authority and do not hide behind explanations of orders received or social morality. Do not please those who command, if someone seeks a follower, do not offer yourselves.

9. Do not launch ambiguous communications about your attitudes and desires. Be loyal to others and say what comes to mind.

10. Speak frankly with those in authority without being hostile or belligerent. Try to keep a balance of your emotions.

Advice for personality 7

1. Don't be impulsive. Observe your impulses and do not give in to them. Exercise control over yourself so you can focus on what benefits you.

2. Learn to listen to others. You will learn new things. Learn to appreciate silence and solitude with the constant noise of TV and music.

3. It is always better to choose quality over quantity, especially in your experiences.

4. Make sure that what you want really benefits you in the long term.

5. Happiness comes from being dedicated to something that was worth the effort. When the priorities are the right ones.

6. Do not make happiness your main goal of life because it will lead you on the wrong path, towards inconsistency and self-centeredness.

7. Do not lose control of yourself, it is easy for this to happen because it is natural for you to be enthusiastic about everything. You are afraid of suffering privation, but if you do not overcome

it, you will inevitably be deprived not only of happiness, but of many other things.

8. It is better to give than to receive.

Advice for personality 8

1. You give your best when you help someone overcome their crisis.

2. You are not the only ones in the world. Others have the same rights and needs that cannot be ignored or violated. If you ignore them people will not only fear you but will lose all respect for you and hate you.

3. Learn to give in, at least occasionally. The desire to always dominate everything and everyone is an indication of an inflated ego: it is a danger signal that will bring you serious conflicts.

4. It is typical of the people to rely only on themselves and not depend on anyone, but ironically they depend on many people, if you all move away you will end up with only servile and treacherous people. Whether in business or in family life, your self-sufficiency is largely illusion.

5. Don't overestimate money as a source of power. Those who feel attracted to you for your money do not love you for yourself and you do not love or respect them.

6. Learn to dedicate yourself to a higher purpose than your personal interest.

7. Giving your family love and receiving it in return is a high purpose. But if it all boils down to your personal interest, you are not spiritually elevated.

8. If you have been ruthless or a cause of pain or offense to others, if you have used people for your pleasure or profit, change your life while you are on time. A life like this leads to a lonely death.

9. One of your potentials is to create opportunities for others. If you create your strength to give hope and prosperity you will be remembered as benefactors and respected.

10. If you meet the needs of others, others will meet your needs.

Advice for personality 9

1. You should examine your tendency to get along with everyone by doing what they want to keep the peace.

2. Don't dream with open eyes. Be part of the world around you. Answer more mentally and emotionally.

3. Be aware that you also have aggressive impulses, anxieties and other feelings that you have to face.

4. Examine your reports and try to see how you helped create the problems. Sacrifice your peace of mind for a moment to get authentic relationships.

5. Practice regular exercise, this is a form of order and self-discipline that you extremely need. Try to gain concentration.

6. Do not repress your feelings or you will somatize with unexplained headaches, back pain, nausea, panic attacks. Seek help if these problems arise.

7. Do not use tranquilizers, they prevent your awareness. Facing the crisis will bring you more self-esteem and will make others understand that you are strong and that they can count on you.

8. Accept life and live it so as not to reach the end of life and feel "never lived".

9. Trust your anxieties to your spouse, your friends. Have confidence and express yourself. This is a basis for peaceful living.

10. Listen to others carefully and learn to know them for what they are.

Living with an awareness of who we are is the only solution for living well in today's sick world. But not only that, there is also much more: knowing one's soul, one's instincts and one's way of doing things is the only solution with which to truly learn to master one's life and therefore to be comfortable with everyone. Choose your life goals and then do everything you need to reach them and if you know yourself it will be much easier.

Self-esteem is something extremely personal and individual and bases both on the beliefs that one has about one's potential, and on those with respect to what others think of us. Never forget that the influence of the other always and in any case exists: the central point is to perceive it as controllable and commensurate with what for me a certain thing is important or not, without, in other words, that it destroys my point of view. The first step in the self-esteem construction process lies in the recognition of one's potential, strengths and virtues. Often this process is blocked or slowed down by the lack of awareness of what universal personal characteristics are worthy of esteem and by the excessive importance given to the judgment of others. Sometimes convincing oneself that one should not be influenced by what others think, becomes an extremely arduous, if not impossible, battle.

This is an important mental mechanism that is often automatic and has strong effects on your everyday life, manifesting itself not only as a pervasive sensation that suffocates every perception of our virtues, but also as a partial belief that even some potentialities are not part of we. In such circumstances it becomes difficult to try to convince ourselves that our thinking is dysfunctional. The best way to overcome this obstacle is not to combat the habitual and linear, albeit dysfunctional, thinking mechanism, which leads us to not see our potential or to realize it only with respect to external meters of value. If, in fact, when we are convinced that we are "lacking" in quality and virtue our self-esteem seems to us totally or partially dependent on the judgment of others, it can be deduced that even the self-esteem of others follows the same path, based, at least apparently and in part, on our judgments. The person we see self-confident, so different from us, is very successful, enjoys our esteem and that of many other people. When we look at a person, we tend to appreciate certain characteristics, especially those that we consider pleasant, worthy of esteem, that create value, that we know are difficult to implement, that, in difficult moments, seem so different from ours, even impossible for us to put in place.

The appreciation of these profound characteristics is guided by a sort of judgment that is formed within us, and this appreciation, in order to be evoked, must satisfy two prerequisites: it must concern something observable and something known, on which it can be expressed an opinion. To be able to estimate something, I have to see the object of my evaluation and have knowledge that allows me to express myself about the value it has for me. If this is true, the fact is equally true that if I respect an individual for certain characteristics, virtues, strengths that belong to him, it means that I am recognizing in the other something that I already know enough to judge as extremely desirable, a characteristic that therefore it belongs to me, even if at a latent and not yet manifest level.

Another wrong perception of oneself concerns one's own abilities. Some people believe they have no value, they have little awareness of their own means: this happens mainly because they pay little attention to observing what happens when they give their best. Maybe when they win a game or when someone pays them a compliment: what is returned to them is positive feedback, yet they can't catch it, they don't listen to it, they close that consideration in a drawer.

Where to start to change one's perception of oneself?

It is essential to do a work on oneself, on a deep part of one's mind. Since this imprinting was written at a deep level in the unconscious, if we want to rewrite it we must reopen the unconscious. To do this work it is important to dialogue with the person's unconscious, through visualizations, through hypnosis (an altered state of consciousness), through specific exercises.

A conscious person is distinguished by the ability to see reality for what it is. He sees not only the positive things or the negative things of himself and the world, but both. Those who are aware of themselves recognize its limits and its strengths: the limits do not frighten it and the strengths do not enhance it. In essence, those with awareness can see the reality of things with extreme balance. Consequently it works its limits and exploits its strengths. Tend from the outside it is recognized because it is comfortable with itself, one has the feeling that that person has found his place in the world and is doing well, he aims to improve himself, but all in all he is well, he is able to accept the present in every shade.

The enneagram is an important starting point of your life that can improve every single day. In fact, only by truly knowing who you are and knowing the answers to your inner questions can you finally make sense of all the unmanageable events that can happen. The people around you will no longer be an insurmountable problem and you can live better in harmony with your soul, the world and all the balance of nature.

If you think this book is a real help, then review Amazon immediately and tell all other people who need this valuable information. Good luck!

Adam